Difford's Guide

365

DAYS OF

Cocktails

Difford's Guide

365 DAYS OF Cocktails

HARPER DESIGN

An Imprint of HarperCollinsPublishers

Contents

Welcome

This book evolved from our Cocktail of the Day on diffordsguide.com, which I was inspired to start during a visit to Barcelona back in 2009. I noticed that many of the old-school cocktail bars such as Ideal, Tandem and Boadas have signs behind the bars that say Cóctel del Día and suggest a cocktail. I asked one bartender why the bar had chosen a particular cocktail to recommend for that day. Disappointingly but honestly, he replied that they had a number of cocktails that they simply rotated.

It occurred to me that with more than three thousand cocktails on our website we should be able to find an appropriate cocktail for each day, influenced by an event, anniversary or celebration. When we started our research, I was struck by the wonderful diversity of days that are celebrated—everything from Smile Power Day to the day that man first walked on the moon—and how interesting many of them are. The background to each day cried out for a short explanation, so we decided to add one, rather than just listing an appropriate cocktail for a certain day.

At the time of writing this book we've run a Cocktail of the Day every day for more than five years on diffordsguide.com and we've picked 365 of the best of those cocktails and date combinations for this book. We hope you'll enjoy reading about each day while sipping the appropriate libation. We've also included some tips for novice cocktail makers, but if you'd like further help, we suggest you watch our how-to videos on the cocktail section of diffordsguide.com.

How to make a cocktail

METHODS

By definition, any drink that is described as a cocktail contains more than one ingredient. So if you are going to make cocktails, you have to know how to combine these various liquids.

As in cooking, there is a correct order in which to do things. With a few exceptions, it runs as follows:

1. Select glass and chill or preheat (if required)
2. Prepare garnish (if required)
3. Pour ingredients into mixing receptacle
4. Add ice (if required)
5. Mix ingredients (shake, stir, blend, etc.)
6. Strain (or pour) into glass
7. Add pre-prepared garnish (if required)
8. Serve to guest or enjoy yourself

Unlike cooking, where there are a myriad of preparation and cooking methods to master, there are essentially only eight different ways to "mix" a cocktail:

1. Build
2. Shake
3. Stir
4. Blend
5. Throw
6. Roll
7. Swizzle
8. Layer

The last, "layering" isn't strictly mixing. On the contrar the idea here is to float each ingredient on its predecesse without the ingredients merging at all—think B52 cocktai At the heart of every cocktail lies at least one of these eigl methods, so understanding these terms is fundamental.

BUILDING

It is common for bartenders and bartending books to sa "build in glass." This simply means to combine ingredien in the glass it is to be served in. This is the usual methc for making highball drinks such as a gin and tonic or whiskey and soda.

SHAKERS AND SHAKING

When you see the phrase "shake with ice and strain," c something similar, in a recipe, you should place all th necessary ingredients with ice cubes in a cocktail shake and shake briskly. Don't be shy about it—imagine how yc might agitate the metal ball in a can of spray paint. Shal for around 15 seconds, then strain the liquid into the glas leaving the ice behind in the shaker. Shaking not only mixe a drink, it also chills, dilutes and aerates it. The dilutic achieved by shaking is just as important to the resultir cocktail as using the right proportions of the ingredients. you use too little ice, it will melt too quickly in the shake producing an overdiluted drink, so fill your shaker at lea two-thirds full with fresh ice.

Losing your grip while shaking is likely to make a me and a flying shaker could injure a bystander, so always hold th shaker firmly with two hands and never shake fizzy ingredien (unless in a minute proportion to the rest of the drink).

RY SHAKE

When making drinks containing cream and eggs, it is common practice among some bartenders to first shake the mixture in shaker without ice, then shake the drink a second time with e. (An increasingly common alternative is to shake with ice st and then again without ice.) This practice is known as ry shaking." The theory is that shaking without ice, and so a higher temperature, allows the drink to emulsify better.

TIRRERS AND STIRRING

irring is one of the most basic ways to mix a cocktail. You ight not give much thought to the technique used to stir a p of tea or even a can of paint, but cocktails deserve a little ore reverence.

Stirring glasses come in a multitude of shapes and sizes. a specially designed lipped mixing glass is not available, a oston glass (the glass half of a Boston shaker) or even the se of a standard shaker will suffice.

There are almost as many different styles of bar aspoons on the market as there are stirring glasses. Some ave spiraling stems, some have flat ends, and others have ree-pronged fork ends. The key thing is for your spoon to ave a long stem so that it will reach down to the base of the ass while allowing you to comfortably hold the stem of the oon high above the mixing glass.

If a cocktail recipe calls for you to "stir with ice and rain," then you should do so.

Measure your ingredients into your chilled stirring glass and then fill it two-thirds with ice.

Hold the bar spoon between your thumb and the first two fingers of your dominant hand, with the spoon's shaft running between your middle finger and ring finger.

Slide the bowl of the spoon down the inside edge of the glass until it almost touches the base of the glass.

- Keeping your arm still, and to an extent your wrist as well, use your fingers to pull the spoon toward and then away from you, aiming to hit the quarter-hour marks on an imaginary clock-face inside your stirring glass. As the spoon runs around, so it will spin the ice and liquid in the glass, while spinning on its own axis in your fingers.

- Stir briskly for about 30 to 45 seconds—this should account for at least 50 revolutions.

- Place your strainer into or over the stirring glass (see "straining") and strain into your chilled serving glass. If the recipe calls for the drink to be served over ice, then you should add ice to your glass first. Never use the ice from the stirring glass in the drink itself.

- The ice used during stirring is now spent and should be dumped, or alternatively can be left in the stirring glass to keep it chilled and ready for the next drink. If you do the latter, remember to dump the ice and rinse the glass with cold water before making the next drink.

STRAINING

When straining a shaken drink, a Hawthorn strainer is usually used, but when straining a stirred drink it is traditional to use a Julep strainer. Both designs of strainer allow the liquid to be poured from the shaker/stirring glass while restraining the spent ice.

Hawthorn strainers have a spring that runs around the circumference to help catch particles of ice and fruit created by the violent act of shaking. They also often have lugs that rest on the rim of the shaker to hold the strainer in position when being used. Most designs of Hawthorn strainers incorporate a ridge or finger rest, which when pushed serves to secure the spring-loaded gap between the strainer and the side of the shaker, allowing finer particles to be caught.

Julep strainers are best described as perforated metal spoons that fit inside the stirring glass. It is said that they take their name from Kentucky gentlemen who historically would hold them over a Mint Julep to keep the ice and mint off their mustaches. Julep strainers are not as efficient at catching small fragments of ice as Hawthorn strainers, but they are more pleasing to use in conjunction with a stirring glass.

FINE STRAINING

Most cocktails that are served straight up—without ice—benefit from an additional strain, over and above the standard Hawthorn strain. This "fine strain" (sometimes also called a "double strain") removes even the smallest fragments of fruit and fine flecks of ice that could float to the surface and spoil the appearance of a drink. Fine straining is not usually necessary when a drink has been stirred, thrown or rolled.

Fine straining is achieved by simply holding a fine sieve, like a tea strainer, between the shaker and the glass.

BLENDING

When a cocktail recipe calls for you to "blend with ice," place all of the ingredients and ice into a blender and blend to a smooth, even consistency. Ideally, you should use crushed ice as this lessens wear on the blender. Place liquid ingredients in the blender first, adding the ice last. If you have a variable-speed blender, always start slowly and build up speed.

THROWING

Throwing offers more dilution and aeration than simply stirring but is gentler than shaking. It is achieved by pouring the ingredients from one container to another from a height so that the cascading liquid pulls air into the drink.

To do this, assemble your ingredients in the base o your shaker. Add ice and strain into a second large-diamete mixing glass/container with a lipped rim, increasing th distance between the two vessels as you pour—alway watch the receptacle you're pouring into, not the one you'r pouring from. Now pour the partially mixed cocktail bac into the first ice-filled container and strain into the secon once again. Repeat this process several times and you wi have "thrown" your drink.

ROLLING

Essentially this is a gentle way of mixing by using a cockta shaker. Fill your shaker in the usual manner and then, instea of shaking, gently roll it end-over-end a few times in a tumblin motion. The best-known example of a drink that benefits fro being rolled rather than shaken is a Bloody Mary. Rollin maintains the thick mouth feel of the tomato juice, wherea shaking tends to produce a Bloody Mary with a thin texture.

SWIZZLING

To swizzle a drink is simply to stir it using a swizzle stick in spinning motion. This style of drink mixing originated in th Caribbean, where originally a twig with a few forked branche was used. Today swizzle sticks are usually made of metal o plastic and have several blades or fingers at right angles to th shaft, although some bartending suppliers still sell Caribbea wooden swizzle sticks.

To swizzle, simply immerse the blades of your swizzl stick into the drink. (Swizzled drinks are served with crushe ice.) Hold the shaft between the palms of both hands an rotate the stick rapidly by sliding your hands back and fort against it. If you do not have a bona fide swizzle stick, use bar spoon in the same manner.

LAYERING

As the name suggests, layered drinks include layers of different ingredients, often in contrasting colors. This effect is achieved by carefully pouring each ingredient into the glass so that it floats on its predecessor.

The success of the technique depends on the density (specific gravity) of the liquids used. As a rule of thumb, the less alcohol and the more sugar an ingredient contains, the heavier it is, so the heaviest ingredients should be poured first and the lightest last. Syrups are nonalcoholic and contain a lot of sugar, so they are usually the heaviest ingredient. Liqueurs, which are higher in sugar and lower in alcohol than spirits, are generally the next heaviest ingredient. The exception is cream and cream liqueurs, which can float.

Layering can be achieved by holding the bowl end of a bar spoon (or a soup spoon) in contact with the side of the glass and over the surface of the drink, then pouring slowly over it. The term "float" refers to layering the final ingredient of a cocktail onto its surface.

MUDDLING

Muddling means pummeling fruits, herbs and/or spices with a muddler (a blunt tool similar to a pestle) to gently crush them and release their flavor. You can also use a rolling pin. Just as you would use a pestle and mortar, push down on the muddler with a twisting action.

Only attempt to muddle in the base of a shaker or a suitably sturdy glass. Never attempt to muddle hard, unripe fruits in a glass as the pressure required could break the glass.

MEASURING

The relative proportion of each ingredient within a cocktail is key to making a great drink. Therefore the accuracy with which ingredients are measured is critical to the finished cocktail.

In this book, we've expressed the measures of each ingredient in "shots." Ideally, a shot is 30 milliliters (1 fluid ounce). Whatever your chosen measuring device, it should have straight sides to enable you to accurately judge fractions of a shot.

ICE

A plentiful supply of fresh ice is essential to making good cocktails. If buying bagged ice, avoid the hollow, tubular kind and thin wafers. Instead, look for large, solid cubes.

When filling ice cube trays, use bottled or filtered water to avoid the taste of chlorine that is often apparent in municipal water supplies. Your ice should be dry, almost sticky to the touch. Avoid "wet" ice that has started to thaw.

Whenever serving a drink over ice, always fill the glass with ice rather than just adding a few cubes. Not only does this make the drink much colder but also the ice lasts longer and so does not dilute the drink.

Never use the same ice in a cocktail shaker twice, even if it's to mix the same drink as before. You should always discard ice after straining the drink and use fresh ice to fill the glass if so required. Pouring the shaken ice into the glass along with the liquid will result in an overly diluted drink that will not be as cold as one where the drink is strained over fresh ice.

CRUSHED ICE

Unless otherwise stated, all references to ice in this book mean cubed ice. If crushed ice is required for a particular recipe, the recipe will state "crushed ice." This is available commercially. Alternatively, you can crush cubed ice in an ice crusher or simply bash it with a rolling pin in a Lewis bag (a thick canvas bag) or wrapped in a tea towel.

INFUSION AND MACERATION

Infusion simply involves immersing whole herbs, spices, nuts or fruit in alcohol and leaving them to soak until the desired flavors have leached out to flavor the alcohol. When macerating, the botanicals being infused are first broken up/ sliced/diced to expose a larger surface area, thereby allowing the alcohol to leach flavor from more of the botanical's cells.

Motion, heat and pressure can be applied to increase the rate of extraction. Motion can be as simple as shaking a bottle in which something is being infused every few hours. (In commercial applications infusion often takes place in revolving tanks.) Heating (leaving in a warm place) helps break open the botanical's cells, thereby allowing the alcohol to more easily extract flavor. Pressure forces the alcohol into the botanical being infused.

Beware of the speed and degree of extraction. A common mistake is to allow overextraction by adding too much of the flavoring substance or leaving it in the alcohol for too long. Tea, for example, infuses very quickly and starts releasing unwanted bitter tannins after just five minutes, while vanilla pods can be left for days and hard substances such as nuts for weeks.

GLASSWARE

Cocktails are something of a luxury—you don't just remove a cap and pour. These drinks take a degree of time and care to mix, so they deserve a decent glass.

Before you start, check that your glassware is clean and free from chips and marks such as lipstick. Always handle glasses by the base or the stem to avoid leaving finger marks, and never put your fingers inside a glass.

CHILLING GLASSES

Ideally, glassware should be chilled in a freezer prior to use. This is particularly important for coupette, martini and flute glasses, in which drinks are usually served without ice. It takes about half an hour to sufficiently chill a glass in the freezer. time is short, you can chill a glass by filling it with ice (ideal crushed, not cubed) and topping it up with water. Leave the glass to cool while you prepare the drink, then discard the ice and water when you are ready to pour. Although this method is quicker than chilling in the freezer, it is not nearly as effective.

PREHEATING GLASSES

To warm a glass for a hot cocktail, place a bar spoon in the glass and fill it with hot water, then discard the water and pour in the drink. Only then should you remove the spoon, which is there to help disperse the shock of the heat.

January

Hair of the Dog

3 teaspoons runny honey
2 shots blended scotch whisky
1 shot whipping cream
1 shot milk

Stir honey with whisky until honey dissolves.
Add other ingredients, shake with ice and strain into
chilled glass. Garnish with grated nutmeg.

NEW YEAR'S DAY AND A BRACING SWIM

Today, thousands of crazy people around the world will jump into freezing cold water. One of the oldest organized New Year swims is in Vancouver, where the Polar Bear Club has been meeting since 1920. As part of a tradition that started in the 1960s, around 10,000 people will charge into the icy North Sea from the beaches of Scheveningen in the Netherlands for the annual Nieuwjaarsduik. Farther west, across the same sea, in South Queensferry, Scotland, crowds will turn out to enjoy the annual "Loony Dook" in which cheery souls in costume parade through the town acting like "loonies" and then take a "dook" in the ice-cold sea. If you're joining them, there's only one thing more to do today —mix a Hair of the Dog.

Zombie

1 teaspoon brown sugar • 1 shot lemon juice • 1 shot golden rum • 1 shot overproof demerara rum
1 shot light white rum • 1 shot pineapple juice • 1 shot lime juice • 1 dash bitters • 1 shot passion fruit syrup

Stir brown sugar with lemon juice in base of shaker until it dissolves. Add other ingredients,
shake with ice and strain into ice-filled glass. Garnish with pineapple wedge.

ANCESTORS' DAY IN HAITI

Haitians celebrated their independence yesterday and today is Ancestors' Day, when they
remember the people who lost their lives in the struggle for Haitian independence. Haitians
today still follow voodoo, a belief system that includes worshipping spirits. Pulp fiction likes to
suggest that Haiti is the home of the zombie, and now you can create your own Zombie. We suggest
you follow Jeff "Beachbum" Berry's reconstruction of Donn the Beachcomber's original recipe, as
featured in Berry's book *Intoxica*. Donn Beach was a Prohibition bootlegger who later owned a chain
of California-based restaurants, bars and nightclubs that are said to have been the first Tiki-style joints.

The Last Straw

1½ shots calvados • 1½ shots elderflower liqueur • 1½ shots medium-dry cider • 1½ shots apple juice

Shake ingredients with ice and strain into ice-filled glass. Garnish with apple slice.

THE DAY THE STRAW WAS INVENTED

Where would the cocktail be without the straw? On this day in 1888, the drinking straw was
patented by Marvin Stone. To start off, it was just hand-rolled paper covered in paraffin.
The oldest drinking straw in existence is a beautiful and precious thing. It was found in a Sumerian
tomb dated 3,000 BC and is a gold tube inlaid with lapis lazuli. One theory is that the Sumerians used
straws to avoid the solid by-products of fermentation at the bottom of their beer. You can celebrate
the creation of this bartending staple with The Last Straw, a cocktail created by Simon Difford in
2006, when he used the last straw behind the bar to sample the first creation of this drink.

Appleissimo

1½ shots apple schnapps liqueur • 2 shots apple juice • 1½ shots cranberry juice • 1½ shots Pernod

Shake first three ingredients with ice and strain into ice-filled glass. Top with Pernod. Garnish with apple slice.

SIR ISAAC NEWTON'S BIRTHDAY

Isaac Newton, who would go on to have one of the greatest brains known to history and to make one of the most important scientific calculations of all time, was born on this day in 1643. Throughout his life, his brilliant curiosity led him to dabble in everything and anything he came across. He was based in the Tower of London for many years as the Master of the Mint, where he waged war against counterfeit money, but most famously he defined gravity after watching an apple falling from a tree. We think it appropriate to mix an Appleissimo, a drink inspired by the very fruit that inspired Newton, and toast the guy who first understood what really keeps our feet on the ground.

Japanese Cocktail

2 shots Cognac V.S.O.P. • ½ shot almond (orgeat) syrup • ¾ shot cold water • 2 dashes bitters

Shake ingredients with ice and strain into chilled glass. Garnish with lemon zest twist.

JOMA SHINJI

The Joma Shinji Japanese New Year archery ritual is based on the Japanese belief that arrows have the power to banish evil—the word *joma* translates as "keep evil spirits away." The ceremony takes place at the Tsurugaoka Hachimangu Shrine in Kamakura and dates back to between 1185 and 1333, when Kamakura was the military capital of Japan. Archers shoot at circular targets 88½ feet away. On the back of a target is painted an upside-down kanji character (a Japanese writing symbol) for "oni," which means "devil." It all seems like a good excuse for us to mix a Japanese-inspired drink, so we're suggesting a Japanese Cocktail. This particular recipe is an adaptation of one that was first published in Jerry Thomas's 1862 book, *Bartender's Guide*.

Epiphany

1¾ shots bourbon whiskey • ½ shot crème de mûre • 2 shots apple juice

Shake ingredients with ice and strain into chilled glass. Garnish with blackberries and strawberry.

THE END OF CHRISTMAS

You may be delighted to know that it's officially the end of Christmas, as today is Epiphany, also known as Three Kings' Day. For the Western Christian church it's the day that the Magis arrived to see the Baby Jesus in the stable, and in the Eastern Christian church it's the day on which Jesus was baptized in the Jordan River. So today in Greece, Cyprus and Bulgaria priests will throw wooden crosses into the sea, a river or a lake and young men will race in to retrieve them. Epiphany also means a moment of sudden or great realization, so our hope for you is that when you mix today's cocktail, an Epiphany, you'll feel full of inspiration for the year to come.

White Russian

2 shots vodka • 1 shot coffee liqueur • 1 shot whipping cream

Shake vodka and coffee liqueur with ice and strain into ice-filled glass. Float lightly whipped cream on top of drink. Garnish with grated nutmeg.

CHRISTMAS DAY IN RUSSIA

Although banned during the Communist era, Christmas is well and truly back now in Russia. Breaking a forty-day Lent period, during which practicing Christians do not eat any meat, Russians usually kick off Christmas festivities on Christmas Eve with a monumental twelve-dish supper. It isn't Santa Claus who delivers presents to Russian children—instead they arrive with Babushka, Grandfather Frost and Grandfather Frost's granddaughter, the Snow Maiden. Today also marks the beginning of Svyatki, an old Slavic holiday in which a young woman would use a mirror and a candle to conjure up the image of her future husband. And, of course, there will be lots of snow, so there's only one drink for today: a snowy White Russian.

Velvet Elvis

1½ shots Tennessee whiskey • 1 shot black raspberry liqueur • ½ shot lime juice
top with lemon or lime soda

Shake first three ingredients with ice and strain into ice-filled glass. Top with lemon or lime soda.
Garnish with lime wedge.

ELVIS PRESLEY BORN

The man who was to become the King of Rock 'n' Roll was born on this day in 1935 in a two-room house in Tupelo, Mississippi. His twin brother, Jessie Garon, was stillborn, leaving Elvis to grow up as an only child. He starred in his first movie, *Love Me Tender*, in 1956 and went on to star in thirty more. It has been estimated that he has sold one billion records, more than anyone in record-industry history. To the man who did so much for rock 'n' roll, we're raising a toast today with a Velvet Elvis: the slightest bit on the sweet side and fruity with a hint of Southern whiskey.

Whiskey Tea Highball

1½ shots bourbon whiskey • ½ shot Islay whisky • ½ shot lapsang souchong sugar syrup
2 shots cold lapsang souchong tea

Stir ingredients with ice and strain into ice-filled glass. Garnish with lemon zest twist.

URBAN CLIMBER ARRESTED

The words *building, edificeering, urban climbing, structuring* and *stegophily* now refer to the act of climbing the outside of a building or an artificial structure, but more than a hundred years ago the concept was brand new and unnamed. One of the first urban climbers, an American named George Gibson Polley, famously known as the Human Fly, was watched by thousands of onlookers on this day in 1920 as he attempted to climb the fifty-seven floors of the Woolworth building in New York City. He was arrested when he reached the thirtieth floor. During his career, Polley climbed more than two thousand buildings and we're guessing he was having quite a ball up there, so today we're toasting him with an appropriately named Whiskey Tea Highball.

Piccadilly Martini

2 shots London dry gin • 1 shot dry vermouth • ⅛ shot absinthe
⅛ shot pomegranate (grenadine) syrup

Shake ingredients with ice and strain into chilled glass. Garnish with orange zest twist.

GOING UNDERGROUND!

The London Underground, and indeed the world's first underground, made its debut on this day back in 1863 as the Metropolitan Railway. It ran gas-lit wooden carriages that were hauled by steam locomotives. Despite a few teething problems, including a sewer flooding the construction works, 38,000 people came out for a ride on the first day. By 1880 the new Tube was carrying 40 million passengers a year. The London Underground continues growing to this day and keeps London ticking. Love it or hate it, it is London, so today we're drinking a Piccadilly Martini to the London Underground and all its staff. This recipe is adapted from one in the 1930 edition of Harry Craddock's *The Savoy Cocktail Book*.

Hot Toddy

1 bar spoon runny honey • 2 shots blended scotch whisky • ½ shot lemon juice
½ shot sugar syrup • 3 cloves • top with boiling water

Place bar spoon loaded with honey in warmed glass. Add other ingredients and stir until honey dissolves. Garnish with lemon slice and cinnamon stick.

HOT TODDY DAY

A hot toddy, hot totty or hot tottie is typically made of liquor, a warm base, usually water, and a sweetener, usually honey or sugar. Its origins are lost in time, but its name may come from an Indian term for palm spirits, and Charles Dickens refers to a toddy in *The Pickwick Papers*. Nowadays, toddies are mainly served as a cure for colds, as honey soothes sore throats and lemon contains vitamin C, but it is actually a fantastic winter warmer and thoroughly deserving of its very own day. So, whether or not you're currently under the weather, why not put on the kettle, crack open a bottle of decent scotch and enjoy Hot Toddy Day.

Frozen Strawberry Daiquiri

2 shots light white rum • ¾ shot lime juice • ½ shot sugar syrup • fresh strawberries

Blend ingredients with 6 oz. of crushed ice. Garnish with whole strawberry.

WE FROZE THE FIRST MAN!

Back in 1967, seventry-three-year-old psychology professor James Bedford became the first person to be cryogenically frozen, in the hope that one day he would be woken up and brought back to life. Robert Nelson, president of the Cryonics Society of California, and one of the three characters involved in his preservation, went on to document the process in the book *We Froze the First Man*. Still cryopreserved to this day, Professor Bedford is stored in liquid nitrogen and has been moved 5 times since the big day. In the cryonics community, the anniversary of Bedford's preservation is celebrated as Bedford Day. If you want to join them, we'd like to suggest you tip your cap to the frozen professor with a Frozen Strawberry Daiquiri.

Country Breeze

2 shots London dry gin • 3½ shots apple juice • ½ shot crème de cassis

Shake ingredients with ice and strain into ice-filled glass. Garnish with strawberry and blueberries.

JOHNNY CASH SINGS IN FOLSOM PRISON

Johnny Cash was arrested seven times, for crimes ranging from smuggling amphetamines from Mexico in his guitar case to picking flowers while trespassing. Cash cultivated his outlaw image, and his empathy with prisoners across America endeared him to them. After releasing the album *Folsom Prison Blues*, Cash was inundated with letters asking him to perform in prisons, and he responded with several performances. The most famous was the one on this day in 1968 when he recorded the album *At Folsom Prison Live*. So, in gratitude to one of the greatest country singers and one of the greatest albums ever, today we'll be drinking a Country Breeze.

Golden Retriever

1 shot light white rum • 1 shot green Chartreuse • 1 shot Licor 43

Stir ingredients with ice and strain into chilled glass. Garnish with orange zest twist.

DRESS UP YOUR PET DAY

As celebrity pet lifestyle expert, animal behaviorist and founder of Dress Up Your Pet Day, Colleen Paige explains, "Today is not a day to disrespect our pets with uncomfortable, vulgar and/or seasonally inappropriate costumes for the sake of a laugh." So today, in all seriousness, to thank our lovely pets for the pleasure and company they bring us, we will be drinking a Golden Retriever, an eminently palatable creation from the great Dick Bradsell.

Treacle No. 1

¼ shot sugar syrup • 2 dashes bitters • 2 shots Jamaican rum • ½ shot apple juice

Stir sugar syrup and bitters with two ice cubes in glass. Add the rum, another couple of ice cubes and stir again. Fill glass with ice and stir again. Finally float apple juice. Garnish with lemon zest twist.

MOLASSES FLOODS BOSTON

Mayhem reigned today in 1919 when a giant tank of molasses, which was awaiting transportation to a distillery for processing into industrial alcohol, exploded in Boston, flattening homes, shops and people with a flood of as much as 2,300,000 gallons of molasses. More than 20 people died and over 150 were injured. The tidal wave of molasses reached around twenty-six feet in height at its peak and moved at over 35 mph, with enough force to warp steel girders. The distiller blamed anarchists, local people blamed negligence, and in the end the distiller settled for around a million dollars, although the area smelled of molasses for years. Today we're pondering that very strange event with a Treacle No. 1.

Nutty Russian

2 shots vodka
1 shot hazelnut liqueur
1 shot coffee liqueur

Stir ingredients with ice and strain into ice-filled glass. Garnish with walnut halves.

IVAN THE TERRIBLE CROWNS HIMSELF TSAR OF RUSSIA

Ivan IV, better known as Ivan the Terrible, is said to have started life mad, and he got madder and madder as the years went on, though it's not surprising, as he was imprisoned in a dungeon by his mother for most of his early life. He was an insatiable reader whose favorite pastimes included rapine, throwing pets out of the upper windows of the Kremlin and weddings—he had seven wives. On the other hand, he was a devout Christian and a champion of the poor and the oppressed. On this day in 1547 he became the first tsar of All the Russias, and during his reign he transformed his country from a small medieval state into a wealthy empire. Because some of his behavior was rather dubious, today we're drinking a Nutty Russian.

Alexander

2 shots London dry gin
1 shot white crème de cacao liqueur
½ shot whipping cream

Shake ingredients with ice and strain into chilled glass. Garnish with grated nutmeg.

PROHIBITION GOES LIVE

At one minute after midnight on this day in 1920, the Volstead Act became law and Prohibition descended on the United States, making it illegal to possess, sell or manufacture drinks with significant alcoholic content. Most saloonkeepers, restaurateurs and drinkers had spent the previous night enjoying as much of the good stuff as they could, often surrounded by funereal black crepe hangings, and perhaps with a ritual coffin passing through. The famous bartender Harry Craddock claimed to have served the last legal cocktail, at the Holland House, on the stroke of midnight on January 16, before taking ship, alongside many other talented American bartenders, for Europe. We are marking this day with an Alexander, a cocktail that was hugely popular in the 1920s.

Honey Bee

3 teaspoons runny honey • 2 shots light white rum • ½ shot lemon juice • ¾ shot cold water

Stir honey with rum in base of shaker until honey dissolves. Add other ingredients, shake with ice and strain into chilled glass. Garnish with lemon zest twist.

WINNIE THE POOH DAY

Today is the birthday of A. A. Milne, who was born in 1882 and went on to create Winnie the Pooh, Piglet and the famous game of Pooh Sticks. If you haven't played Pooh Sticks (though you probably have, even if you called it something else), this is how you play: two or more people stand on the upstream side of a bridge, each with a carefully chosen and well-memorized stick. On the word everyone drops their stick into the water and rushes to the other side of the bridge—the first stick to appear from under the bridge is the winner. To mark the birthday of A. A. Milne, we'll be enjoying Pooh's favorite and only item of consumption—honey—and remembering his many hilarious adventures with a Honey Bee.

Southern Mint Cobbler

7 fresh mint leaves • 2 shots Southern Comfort • ½ shot lemon juice • ½ shot peach purée

Lightly muddle mint (just to bruise) in base of shaker. Add other ingredients, shake with ice and strain into glass filled with crushed ice. Garnish with mint.

JANIS JOPLIN'S BIRTHDAY

Janis Joplin died at the age of twenty-seven, soon after Brian Jones and Jimi Hendrix. Hard-living, hard-partying and tormented, and a painter as well as a singer, Joplin was born in Texas on this day in 1943. Her performances at Monterey, at Woodstock and aboard the Festival Express train made her a counterculture icon, while her take on "Piece of My Heart" still makes the lists of the all-time greatest rock songs. She was immortalized by her lover Leonard Cohen, who wrote "Chelsea Hotel #2" for her. Janis's favorite legal high was Southern Comfort—she would often take a swig from a bottle onstage. We think that, as a girl from the South, she might have liked a nice, cooling Southern Mint Cobbler, which adds peach, lemon juice and mint to her preferred spirit.

Americana

1 cube granulated sugar • 4 dashes bitters • ½ shot bourbon whiskey • top with champagne brut

Coat sugar cube with bitters and drop into glass. Pour bourbon and then champagne into chilled glass. Garnish with apple slice.

HELLO, MR. PRESIDENT

The presidential Inauguration Day was originally on March 4, and in the early days the ceremony was a fairly simple event—George Washington's speech, for example, was just 135 words long. Inauguration Day was changed by statute in 1933, and every four years, on this day in January, on a day that is set by law, a new president is sworn in. The event follows Election Day, which is always the Tuesday after the first Monday in November. Over the years Inauguration Day has grown and grown and now includes days of parades, prayers and presentations. What else could we drink today but an Americana?

Triple Orange

1 shot vodka • 1 shot Grand Marnier • ¼ shot Campari • 1½ shots orange juice • ½ fresh egg white

Shake ingredients with ice and strain into chilled glass. Garnish with orange zest twist.

LADY OF ALTAGRACIA DAY

Altagracia, who is the patron saint of the Dominican Republic, is based on an interpretation of the Virgin Mary. One of the many stories about Altagracia suggests that a portrait of her repeatedly disappeared from a house, only to keep turning up in an orange tree. Another story comes from a book called *The Gift of Gracias*, and explains how the Lady of Altagracia saved a family's farm through an abundant orange harvest. Whichever story you prefer, it can generally be agreed that the festival is associated with oranges, and we feel that a Triple Orange not only reflects this but is a delicious cocktail as well.

Wine Cooler

2 shots Sauvignon Blanc white wine
½ shot citrus vodka • ½ shot lemon juice
½ shot orange juice
top with lemon or lime soda

Shake first four ingredients with ice and strain into ice-filled glass. Top with soda and lightly stir. Garnish with orange slice.

THE PATRON SAINT OF WINEMAKERS

Happy Saint's Day to St. Vincent of Saragossa, patron saint of winemakers and vine dressers! Born in France, St. Vincent became deacon of Saragossa in Aragon, Spain, under the reign of the Roman emperor Diocletian. Like many martyrs of the time, he was tortured hideously and then thrown into the sea, where his remains were cast up on a promontory now known as Cape St. Vincent. Quite how this prepared him to protect the vintners of the world we do not know, but after all that, we're sure he'd have needed a Wine Cooler, which is what we're drinking today.

Mississippi Punch

1½ shots bourbon whiskey
¾ shot Cognac V.S.O.P.
¾ shot lemon juice
1 shot sugar syrup • 2 shots cold water

Shake ingredients with ice and strain into glass filled with crushed ice. Garnish with a lemon slice.

FIRST BRIDGE ACROSS THE MISSISSIPPI

We're particularly fond of New Orleans because it's home to Tales of the Cocktail, the world's premier annual cocktail festival. One of the defining features of New Orleans is the Mississippi River, so today we'd like to drink a toast to the first bridge to span the Mississippi with Mississippi Punch. The original bridge was quite a quirky sight and started out as a toll bridge on this very day in 1855. Now in its fourth incarnation, the bridge's official name is the Father Louis Hennepin Bridge, after Louis Hennepin, the 17th-century explorer who discovered Saint Anthony Falls a little way downstream.

Churchill Martini

2½ shots London dry gin

Stir gin with ice while glancing at an unopened bottle of dry vermouth. Strain into chilled glass. Garnish with olive.

ANNIVERSARY OF WINSTON CHURCHILL'S DEATH

You have to admire the style of a man who not infrequently directed World War II from his bath, with a glass of champagne in hand. A fan of Johnnie Walker, martinis, champagne, fine wines and cognac, Churchill when rebuked by Lady Astor for drunkenness shot back, "Yes, Madam. But you are ugly and in the morning I shall be sober." He also famously said that the only way to make a martini was with ice-cold gin and a bow in the direction of France. For best Churchillian style, enjoy your Churchill Martini in the bath while smoking a cigar.

Bobby Burns

2 shots blended scotch whisky
1 shot sweet vermouth
¼ shot Drambuie
2 dashes Peychaud's Bitters

Stir ingredients with ice and strain into chilled cocktail glass. Garnish with lemon zest twist.

BURNS NIGHT

Scots everywhere will be holding Burns Suppers tonight in honor of the birth of Scotland's favorite poet and son, Robert Burns, who was born today in 1759. One of seven children, he composed "Ode to a Haggis," which will be recited as the haggis is cut tonight, the New Year song "Auld Lang Syne" and "Scots Wha Hae," which served for a long time as the unofficial Scottish anthem. We hope that you'll be digging all things tartan out of your closet, prepping a haggis and finding some bagpipe music for the celebrations, but if not, this is still the perfect excuse to crack open a bottle of whisky, pour a little over the haggis, have a dram on the rocks…and enjoy the rest of it in a Bobby Burns cocktail. This version is adapted from David Embury's 1953 *Fine Art of Mixing Drinks*.

Shandygaff

Fill glass ⅔ with Pilsner lager • ginger ale

Pour ale into glass, top with ginger ale.

NATIONAL AUSTRALIA DAY

Today is the anniversary of the first fleet of convict ships arriving at Sydney Cove in 1788, and the day will be spent celebrating everything that is great about Australia and being Australian. It wasn't until 1994 that all the states and territories in Australia celebrated Australia Day as a unified public holiday, and since then the day has grown and grown. If you're lucky enough to be in Australia, then your day will be all about barbecues, outdoor concerts and beer. We suggest you take yours in a Shandygaff, a beer and ginger ale combination that dates back to at least the late 19th century.

Leninade

1½ shots citrus vodka • ½ shot triple sec • ¾ shot lemon juice
½ shot pomegranate (grenadine) syrup • 2 dashes orange bitters • top with soda

Shake first 5 ingredients with ice and strain into ice-filled glass. Top with soda. Garnish with lemon slice.

SIEGE OF LENINGRAD BROKEN

At last, on this day in 1944, the Soviet army broke through the German blockade of Leningrad, which had endured for an agonizing 872 days. All land communication had been cut off, the city had been subjected to air and artillery bombardment, and hundreds of thousands of Leningrad's population of 2.5 million had died since the beginning of the siege on September 1, 1941. The harshest winter in decades had added to their suffering, which had been eased a little when Lake Ladoga to the north of the city froze, allowing an ice road to bring in supplies. In memory of the heroes who freed the city, and those who endured so much, today we will be drinking a Leninade.

Serendipity

6 fresh blackberries • 1 shot London dry gin • ½ shot vanilla liqueur • 3 shots cranberry juice
¼ shot lemon juice • ¼ shot sugar syrup • ½ shot crème de cassis

Muddle blackberries in base of shaker. Add other ingredients, shake with ice and strain into glass filled with crushed ice. Garnish with mint.

INVENTION OF THE WORD *SERENDIPITOUS*

Serendipity means a fortunate happenstance or pleasant surprise. Well, our cheerful discovery is that, because this word was first used on this day in 1754 in a letter written by Horace Walpole, we can all today enjoy a Serendipity cocktail. Walpole was describing to a friend an unexpected discovery he had made by referring to a Persian fairy tale, "The Three Princes of Serendip." The princes, he wrote, were "always making discoveries, by accidents and sagacity, of things which they were not in quest of."

Victorian Lemonade

12 fresh mint leaves • 1½ shots London dry gin • 1 shot lemon juice
¾ shot sugar syrup • 2½ shots cold water

Lightly muddle mint (just to bruise) in base of shaker. Add other ingredients, shake with ice and strain into ice-filled glass. Garnish with lemon slice.

THE VICTORIA CROSS WAS ESTABLISHED

It was on this day in 1856 that Queen Victoria established the Victoria Cross—the highest award that a British or Commonwealth serviceman can receive. It is awarded for most conspicuous bravery, or some daring or preeminent act of valor or self-sacrifice, or extreme devotion to duty in the presence of the enemy. In the years that Victoria Crosses have been available, an average of about nine have been awarded per year. However, twenty-four were awarded in a single day for bravery in the relief of Lucknow during the Indian Mutiny (1857), and only fourteen have been awarded since World War II. Tonight, why not mix a Victorian Lemonade and drink to Victoria Cross recipients and their heroism?

Claret Cobbler

1½ shots Cognac V.S.O.P. • 1 shot Grand Marnier • 2½ shots Shiraz wine

Shake ingredients with ice and strain into glass filled with crushed ice. Garnish with mint.

CHARLES I BEHEADED

The last regal walk of Charles I was in London, from St. James's Palace to the Banqueting House and thence out of an upstairs window on to a scaffold. It was bitterly cold that January day in 1649 and Charles had asked his valet for extra underclothes, as he was concerned that the crowd would interpret any shivering as a sign of fear. Charles had stammered all his life but this affliction left him in his last days, and both his bearing at the trial and his conduct on the scaffold were to transform him from an impossible king into a royal martyr. His last meal was a piece of dry bread and a cup of claret. Who knows, but had his chaplain, Dr. Juxon, known of our Claret Cobbler, he might have insisted on its warming attributes.

South Pacific Breeze

1½ shots London dry gin • ¾ shot Galliano L'Autentico liqueur
top with lemonade • ¾ shot blue curaçao liqueur

Pour gin and Galliano L'Autentico liqueur into ice-filled glass. Top with lemonade to just below the rim. Drizzle blue curaçao liqueur around top of drink. Garnish with pineapple wedge.

NAURU INDEPENDENCE DAY

Formerly known as Pleasant Island, Nauru is a country of only eight square miles in the South Pacific, and a population of 9,378, making it the second-smallest state by population in the world (Vatican City is the smallest). First inhabited by Micronesian and Polynesian people at least three thousand years ago, Nauru gained its independence from a United Nations trusteeship on this day in 1968. The twelve-pointed star on the country's flag represents the twelve clans or tribes of the island, and ancestry here is traced through the maternal line. Today, mix yourself a South Pacific Breeze, close your eyes and try to imagine you're lazing under a palm tree on a sandy Nauru beach.

February

Ice White Cosmo

2 shots vodka
¾ shot ice wine
1¼ shots white cranberry juice
¼ shot lime juice

Shake ingredients with ice and strain into chilled glass. Garnish with orange zest.

THE LAST FROST FAIR ON THE THAMES

Today in 1814 the River Thames finally froze solid enough for Londoners to enjoy their last-ever frost fair. Someone led an elephant across the river at Blackfriars to show that the ice was safe to walk on; shopkeepers set up tents to sell brandy, beer, wine and gin; and someone set up an open fire, roasted a sheep on it and sold it as "Lapland mutton." When the ice melted a few days later, it was the end of an era. Victorian engineering changed the flow of the river, and the Thames would never freeze again. We are commemorating the great fair with an aptly named Ice White Cosmo.

Fog Cutter

1½ shots light white rum • ¾ shot Cognac V.S.O.P. • ½ shot London dry gin • 1½ shots orange juice • ½ shot lemon juice • ½ shot almond (orgeat) syrup • ½ shot amontillado sherry

Shake first six ingredients with ice and strain into ice-filled glass. Float sherry on top of drink. Garnish with orange wedge.

GROUNDHOG DAY

Groundhog Day is an old tradition that dates back to central European legends about Candlemas, when bears might emerge from hibernation, signaling the end of winter. In Pennsylvania, where many German immigrants settled, the focus of the legend became the groundhog. The story goes that if the groundhog wakes from its hibernation to find cloudy weather, it won't see its shadow and spring will begin. If it is a sunny day, the groundhog will be freaked by its own shadow and return to the dark, meaning that winter will last another six weeks. We are drinking a Fog Cutter, and for once hoping for a cloudy day.

American Pie Martini

1½ shots bourbon whiskey
½ shot apple schnapps liqueur
½ shot crème de myrtille liqueur
¾ shot cranberry juice
½ shot apple juice
¼ shot lime juice

Shake ingredients with ice and strain into chilled glass. Garnish with apple slice.

THE DAY THE MUSIC DIED

February 3, 1959, is known to 1950s addicts as "the day the music died," a day immortalized in Don McLean's early 1970s song "American Pie." Why today? A plane fell out of the sky, only a short distance from the airport, taking with it rock 'n' roll pioneers Buddy Holly, Ritchie Valens and the Big Bopper (J. P. Richardson). So today we are raising a glass to Buddy, a bespectacled guy who overcame physical disability to become one of the biggest stars of the 1950s, with an American Pie Martini.

Chinese Cosmopolitan

2 shots spiced honey liqueur
¾ shot lychee liqueur
½ shot lime juice
1 shot red cranberry juice

Shake ingredients with ice and strain into chilled glass. Garnish with orange zest twist.

CHINESE NEW YEAR

The Chinese New Year is thousands of years old, and its date is dictated by the lunar calendar. There are twelve different animals that represent the different years in the Chinese zodiac. Traditional celebrations include family gatherings, giving money in red paper envelopes and fireworks. One of the best celebrations so far must have been the dancing dragon on February 19, 2000, which was about 10,000 feet long, and was brought to life by 3,200 people on the Great Wall of China. A big part of the Chinese New Year is about wiping out all grudges and wishing peace and happiness to everybody. So what better way to do it than mixing a Chinese Cosmopolitan for your friends and family to celebrate with tonight?

Bacardi Special

1½ shots light white rum
¾ shot London dry gin
½ shot lime juice
¼ shot pomegranate (grenadine) syrup
⅛ shot sugar syrup
½ shot cold water

Shake ingredients with ice and
strain into chilled glass. Garnish with
maraschino cherry.

BACARDI ESTABLISHED

The founder of Bacardi was a Catalan wine merchant named Facundo Bacardí Massó, who left Spain for Cuba in 1830, where he got into rum big time. Eventually, on this day in 1862, Facundo and his brother José set up shop in a Santiago de Cuba distillery, where Bacardi was started. Along with Henri Schueg, the brothers branded Cuba as the home of rum. The rest, as they say, is history. Join us in celebrating this giant of a brand with a Bacardi Special—a cocktail adapted from Harry Craddock's *The Savoy Cocktail Book.*

Chocolate Sazerac

½ shot absinthe
2 shots bourbon whiskey
½ shot white crème de cacao liqueur
¼ shot sugar syrup
2 dashes Peychaud's Bitters

Fill glass with ice, pour in absinthe, top up with water and leave the mixture to stand. Separately stir bourbon, cacao, sugar and bitters with ice. Finally, discard contents of glass (absinthe, water and ice) and strain contents of shaker into empty absinthe-coated glass.

WORLD NUTELLA DAY

Is Nutella one of your guilty pleasures? If so, today is for you. For the hazelnut spread known as Nutella has its very own unofficial celebration day today: World Nutella Day. Organizers recommend doing anything you can think of with Nutella, from making art with it to eating it straight from the jar with a spoon. As we do like a bit of chocolate in a cocktail from time to time, we are marking the occasion with an adequately adult Chocolate Sazerac.

Queen Martini

1½ shots London dry gin
½ shot dry vermouth
½ shot sweet vermouth
½ shot orange juice
½ shot pineapple juice

Shake ingredients with ice
and strain into chilled glass.

ELIZABETH WINDSOR BECOMES QUEEN

Queen Elizabeth II is the second living monarch to achieve a Diamond Jubilee. In 1952 her father, George VI, died in his sleep at Sandringham House, having reigned for only fifteen years. Elizabeth heard the news in Treetops, a safari lodge in Kenya, where she had been sleeping in a tree house while on a tour of Africa. She was the first British royal to become monarch while out of the country, and, obviously, the first to do so in a tree house. We are toasting Her Majesty with a cocktail fit for a queen.

Dickens's Dry Martini

2½ shots London dry gin
½ shot dry vermouth

Stir ingredients with ice and strain
into chilled glass.

CHARLES DICKENS'S BIRTHDAY

Charles John Huffam Dickens was born on this very day back in 1812. Despite describing himself as a "very small and not-over-particularly-taken-care-of boy," he went on to write fifteen novels and become one of Britain's best-loved authors. To celebrate the famous Londoner, we're recommending a couple of London drinking dens. Why not try out The George Inn on Borough High Street in Southwark, which is mentioned in *Little Dorrit*, or another classic Dickensian watering hole, Ye Olde Cheshire Cheese, on Fleet Street, from *A Tale of Two Cities*. And when you get there, try ordering a Dickens's Dry Martini!

Monkey Gland

2 shots London dry gin
1½ shots orange juice
⅛ teaspoon absinthe
⅛ shot pomegranate (grenadine) syrup
⅛ shot sugar syrup

Shake ingredients with ice
and strain into chilled glass. Garnish
with orange zest twist.

H. MACELHONE BUYS NEW YORK

Today in 1923 Harry MacElhone finally achieved his dream and bought the New York Bar on 5 Rue Daunou, Paris. One of the very, very few bars to have remained in the same family for three generations, Harry's New York Bar has played host to some of the world's best bartenders and most notorious guests, from Hemingway to Sartre. We will be toasting Harry, and his bar, with one of the few cocktails that all sources agree he created, the Monkey Gland.

Absolutely Fabulous

1 shot vodka
2 shots cranberry juice
top with champagne brut

Shake first two ingredients with ice and strain into glass. Top with champagne. Garnish with strawberry.

THE BEATLES INVADE AMERICA

On this day in 1964, the Beatles officially cracked America—making them still one of the very few British bands to have achieved this difficult feat. More than seventy-three million Americans, a vast chunk of the population, tuned in to watch them perform live on *The Ed Sullivan Show*. The legendary host of the TV variety show had been passing through London when his plane was delayed by a gaggle of screaming girls. Wondering what all the fuss was about, Ed came across the Beatles. We're toasting the Fab Four with an Absolutely Fabulous.

Grand Designs

Sprig of rosemary • 1½ shots London dry gin • 1 shot elderflower liqueur
¼ shot dry vermouth • ¾ shot pineapple juice

Muddle rosemary in base of shaker. Add other ingredients, shake with ice and strain into chilled glass.
Garnish with rosemary sprig.

DEATH OF COCO CHANEL

Gabrielle Bonheur "Coco" Chanel led an extraordinary life. She introduced clothing staple such as bell-bottoms and peacoats to women around the world, and was the only couturier to be included in Time's 100 Most Important People of the Century list. When Gabrielle's mother died she spent six years in an orphanage, where she learned to be a seamstress. After a brief stin as a cabaret singer, she met a young French textile heir and became his mistress, simultaneously falling in love with diamonds, dresses and pearls. She had other affairs, but her true marriage wa always to her label. Mix up a Grand Designs today as a toast to the queen of French fashion and the epitome of elegance.

Bénédictine Conversion

2 shots tequila • ½ teaspoon mezcal • ¼ shot Bénédictine D.O.M. liqueur
¼ shot white crème de cacao liqueur • ¾ shot cold water

Stir ingredients with ice and strain into chilled glass.

POPE BENEDICT XVI RETIRES

On this day in 2013, Pope Benedict became the first pope to resign since Gregory XII in 1415, and the first to do so of his own initiative since 1294. While most popes carry on till the day they die, Benedict decided that his declining health meant he needed to step aside. Serving as pope from April 2005, the former Joseph Ratzinger was ordained as a priest in 1951 in his native Bavaria. Now known as Pope Emeritus, Benedict retains the style of His Holiness, and the title of pope, and continues to dress in papal white. We're toasting his good sense in knowing when enough is enough with a suitably religious benediction: the classic combination of Bénédictine D.O.M and brandy.

Pisco Sour

2 shots pisco • ¾ shot lime juice • ½ shot sugar syrup • ½ fresh egg white • 1 dash orange flower water

Shake ingredients with ice and strain into chilled glass. Garnish with three drops of Angostura bitters.

FOUNDING OF SANTIAGO

Spanish conquistador Pedro de Valdivia stood on Huelén Hill (now known as Cerro Santa Lucía) today in 1541 and conducted a founding ceremony for the city of Santiago, Chile's capital. The site was chosen for its climate and its lush vegetation, though there were initially quite a few teething problems when the local inhabitants didn't take too kindly to the Spanish invasion. But within about twenty years, the settlement was stabilized—nowadays, there are more than five million people living in Santiago. There's no way that a South American celebration could take place without the presence of pisco, so we're suggesting what is, arguably, Chile's national drink … mix a Pisco Sour tonight and raise a glass to Santiago—its past, present and future.

Pink Palace

2 shots London dry gin • ½ shot Grand Marnier • ½ shot lime juice
¼ shot pomegranate (grenadine) syrup

Shake ingredients with ice and strain into chilled glass. Garnish with lemon zest twist.

BARBIE GOES ON SALE

From a humble toy manufacturer came one of the world's biggest brands, Barbie, or to give the doll her full name, Barbara Millicent Roberts. Barbie was conceived by Ruth Handler when she noticed her daughter giving adult characters to her dolls, who in those days were all modeled on children. Ruth's husband was a cofounder of the Mattel toy company, which still produces Barbie and her extended family. The first Barbie doll was sold today in 1959, wearing a black-and-white zebra-striped swimsuit and signature topknot ponytail, and was available as either a blonde or a brunette. We're toasting more than half a century of playtime with Barbie by mixing a Pink Palace, a drink we're sure Barbara would enjoy.

Honey Bee Mine

3 teaspoons runny honey
2 shots light white rum
⅛ shot vanilla extract
¾ shot champagne brut

Stir honey with rum in base of shaker to dissolve honey. Add vanilla extract, shake with ice and strain into chilled glass. Top with champagne. Garnish with honeycomb.

VALENTINE'S DAY

You can't have failed to notice that it's St. Valentine's Day, a time of year when a sum equivalent to the GDP of a small country is spent on red roses, fancy chocolates and enormous, novelty padded cards. But who exactly was St. Valentine? Valentinus, to give him his proper name, was supposedly a saint who lived in third-century Italy. Imprisoned for performing weddings for young soldiers who were forbidden to marry, and for ministering to Christians, he was apparently executed on February 14, 269. He inspired an entire tradition by penning the first "Valentine's card" the night before he was executed. It was to his jailer's daughter and signed "your Valentine." Around 1,200 years later, the royal court in England turned the saint's day into a ritual of courtly love, and it has remained so ever since. Why not impress your loved one with a Valentine's cocktail by mixing them a Honey Bee Mine?

Maple Leaf

2 shots bourbon whiskey • ½ shot lemon juice • ⅓ shot maple syrup

Shake ingredients with ice and strain into ice-filled glass. Garnish with lemon zest twist.

CANADA FLAG DAY

Today is the day that Canada adopted its iconic flag, and the maple leaf became the symbol of Canada. The Canadian politician Maurice Bourget said, "The flag is the symbol of the nation's unity, for it, beyond any doubt, represents all the citizens of Canada without distinction of race, language, belief or opinion." Which is surely enough to get everyone, Canadian or otherwise, reaching for the maple syrup … so mix up a Maple Leaf and raise a glass to "O Canada" today.

King's Jubilee

2 shots light white rum • ¾ shot maraschino liqueur • ½ shot lemon juice

Shake ingredients with ice and strain into chilled glass. Garnish with lemon zest twist.

TUTANKHAMUN'S TOMB UNSEALED

In front of an audience of dignitaries from around the world, on this day in 1923, the archaeologist Howard Carter opened the tomb of King Tutankhamun, revealing a blaze of gold, jewels and leopard-print accessories and launching any number of horror movies. Mercifully, after a previous unveiling of a different tomb had gone wrong, as tomb robbers had gotten there first, Carter had checked that there would be something to see when they got there. We are marking the occasion with a King's Jubilee.

Opera

2 shots London dry gin
¼ shot maraschino liqueur
2 shots Dubonnet Red
3 dashes orange bitters

Shake ingredients with ice and strain into chilled glass. Garnish with orange zest twist.

PREMIERE OF
MADAMA BUTTERFLY

Today in 1904, the La Scala opera house in Milan saw the grand opening of *Madama Butterfly*. It did not go well. Despite an all-star cast and Giacomo Puccini as the composer, there hadn't been enough time to rehearse and the heart-wrenching opera was a flop. However, Puccini made some modifications, including chopping the second act in half to create a three-act production, and re-unveiled his masterpiece on May 28 in Brescia, where it was a huge success. We're toasting Puccini's genius with an aptly named Opera.

Bloody Mary

½ ring yellow bell pepper
2 shots vodka • 3 shots tomato juice
½ shot sherry amontillado
½ shot lemon juice • ¼ shot sugar syrup
2 pinches celery salt
3 grinds black pepper • 10 drops Tabasco
4 dashes Worcestershire sauce

Muddle pepper in base of shaker. Add other ingredients, roll rather than shake with ice and strain into ice-filled glass. Grate pepper over drink. Garnish with celery stick.

PETIOT'S BIRTHDAY

Born in Paris today in 1900, Fernand "Pete" Petiot would become famous as the inventor of the Bloody Mary. Petiot was passionate about all things hospitality, and wherever he worked, he was known for his sense of humor and his way with customers and other bartenders. Did he invent the Bloody Mary cocktail? Quite possibly not—but he almost certainly did shape the combo of vodka and tomato juice into something close to its current spicy form. We're toasting him with a Bloody Mary.

White Lady Cocktail

1½ shots London dry gin
¾ shot triple sec • ¾ shot lemon juice
⅓ shot sugar syrup • ½ fresh egg white

Shake ingredients with ice and strain back into the same shaker to remove the ice. Then dry shake and strain into chilled glass. Garnish with lemon zest twist.

THE FEMININE MYSTIQUE
IS RELEASED

When Betty Friedan published today in 1963 *The Feminine Mystique*, a book that would reach an audience of millions, she changed lives. None of what Friedan said would seem to be rocket science today. She claimed that millions of housewives were unhappy with their lives and wanted more than to simply keep their men and children happy. And she argued that it was okay not only to want more but also to pursue more, making her an icon of the feminist movement. Working women of all persuasions owe Friedan a great debt of gratitude, and we are toasting her with a White Lady Cocktail.

Ballet Russe

2 shots vodka • ¾ shot crème de cassis
1 shot lime juice • ¼ shot sugar syrup

Shake ingredients with ice
and strain into chilled glass. Garnish
with lime wedge.

PREMIERE OF TCHAIKOVSKY'S BALLET *SWAN LAKE*

Tonight in 1877 Tchaikovsky's *Swan Lake* premiered at the Bolshoi theater in Moscow. The story was fashioned from Russian folk stories and tells the tale of Odette, a princess turned into a swan by an evil sorcerer's curse. The ballet many of us see nowadays, however, is based both choreographically and musically on the 1895 revival, although there have been many modern interpretations since then, most notably Matthew Bourne's, which had men take the traditional female roles. In thanks for this beautiful ballet, we're toasting Tchaikovsky with a Ballet Russe.

Celtic Margarita

2 shots blended scotch whisky
1 shot triple sec • 1 shot lemon juice

Shake ingredients with ice and strain
into chilled glass. Salt rim. Garnish with
lemon wedge.

BOUDICCA'S BODY FOUND

It was on this day back in 1988 that Britain's *Daily Telegraph* newspaper reported that contractors working on Platform 10 at King's Cross station had unearthed the skeleton of the warrior Queen Boudicca. Was it really her? Who knows. There's a lot of mystery surrounding this queen of the Iceni tribe—in particular her death and burial place. Historians have estimated that she died around AD 60, when it's thought that she poisoned herself to avoid capture by the Romans. Actually, several people have claimed to have found Boudicca's burial site—but all in different locations. We're choosing today to celebrate the Celtic queen by mixing up a Celtic Margarita.

Tommy's Margarita

2 shots tequila • 1 shot lime juice
½ shot agave syrup

Shake ingredients with ice and strain into
chilled glass. Garnish with lime wedge.

MARGARITA DAY

There are days for most things in the United States, but Margarita Day is one that is very close to our hearts. No matter who invented this classic cocktail, or added a salt rim to a Picador, which is arguably the precursor to this drink, the Margarita is a seriously underrated cocktail. For those in the northern hemisphere, February is a little cold for a frozen Margarita, but no weather is too chilly or too warm for a Tommy's Margarita, made with agave syrup in lieu of the usual triple sec. If you haven't tried this phenomenal variation, we strongly recommend you do so today.

FEBRUARY 23

Russian Qualuude

½ shot Galliano L'Autentico liqueur
½ shot green Chartreuse
½ shot vodka

Refrigerate ingredients, then layer in chilled glass by carefully pouring in the order listed.

DEFENDER OF THE FATHERLAND DAY

Pozdravlyayu! Today marks the date that the first masses were drafted into the Red Army during the Russian Civil War, 1918. The day is now celebrated in Russia as the patriotically named Defender of the Fatherland Day. The Russian festival is still focused around serving troops and military veterans, but it has grown into a big celebration, which provides an excuse for everyone to have a party. Traditionally, women give presents and cards to Russian men, and there are parades to honor the military. Pour a Russian Qualuude shot tonight for Russia. *Na zdorovje!*

FEBRUARY 24

Tiki Max

1 shot navy rum • 1 shot light white rum
½ shot Grand Marnier • ½ shot apricot brandy liqueur • ¾ shot almond (orgeat) syrup • ¾ shot lime juice • 1½ shots pineapple juice • ½ shot orange juice
6 dashes bitters • ½ shot overproof rum

Shake first nine ingredients with ice and strain into glass filled with crushed ice. Float overproof rum on drink. Garnish with pineapple, orange wedges and mint.

THE CALENDAR'S BIRTHDAY

Today in 1572 Pope Gregory XIII shortened the year by ten minutes, forty-eight seconds— and the Gregorian calendar was born. The old calendar, inherited from Julius Caesar, allowed for precisely 365¼ days a year, with a leap year every four years. That left almost eleven minutes a year unaccounted for. So Gregory added ten days to the current date, and made each year that is exactly divisible by four a leap year. Thinking of the ticking clock, we're drinking a Tiki Max.

FEBRUARY 25

Fly Like a Butterfly

1 shot dry vermouth
1 shot sweet vermouth
½ shot Dubonnet Red
½ shot orange juice

Shake ingredients with ice and strain into chilled glass. Garnish with orange zest twist.

CASSIUS CLAY BECOMES WORLD CHAMPION

The man we now know as Muhammad Ali, but who was born Cassius Clay, won a surprise victory over the legendary Sonny Liston today in 1964, to became world heavyweight boxing champion. Despite four years out of competition, Ali earned his title "The Greatest." He became a hero of the civil rights movement, has founded humanitarian awards and has helped perceptions of Islam in his country immensely. Famous for his "float like a butterfly, sting like a bee" strategy, The Greatest still battles on, and we're toasting him today with a Fly Like a Butterfly.

Grand Berry

4½ shots cranberry juice • ¼ shot lime juice • 1½ shots Grand Marnier

Pour cranberry juice into ice-filled glass to half full. Add lime juice and Grand Marnier.
Garnish with strawberry, raspberries and lime wedges.

THE GRAND CANYON IS SAFE

One of the world's most beautiful natural wonders was designated a national park by Congress on this day in 1919. The formation of the Grand Canyon National Park is thought by many to be one of the earliest successes of the environmental conservation movement—without this status it's possible that a dam might have been constructed along the course of the Colorado River. The breathtaking one-mile-deep gorge of the Grand Canyon, with its stunning striations of color, was formed as the Colorado River eroded through the uplifted Colorado Plateau. A cranberry-based Grand Berry doesn't look quite as marvelous as the Grand Canyon at sunset but its lovely red color does go some way in that direction.

Snowfall Cocktail

*¼ whole vanilla pod • 1½ shots vanilla-infused vodka • 1½ shots whipping cream
½ shot sugar syrup*

Cut vanilla pod along its length and muddle in base of shaker. Add other ingredients.
Garnish with vanilla pod.

INTERNATIONAL POLAR BEAR DAY

Polar bears are majestic and pretty fearsome creatures that also happen to produce the most adorable-looking offspring known to the Arctic Circle. Today is about raising awareness for their perilous situation as the ice recedes, leaving them with less land and, therefore, less food. Today politicians and environmentalists campaign for everyone to use energy more conservatively and lessen our carbon footprints. For the remaining 20,000 or so bears, we're marking today with a Snowfall Cocktail.

Dry Martini #4

2½ shots London dry gin • ⅓ shot dry vermouth

Stir ingredients with ice and strain into chilled glass. Garnish with stuffed olive.

GOOD-BYE, FAREWELL AND AMEN

Viewing figures for the final episode of the TV series *M*A*S*H* broke the record that had been set by the *Dallas* "Who Shot J.R.?" episode. This made it the most-watched TV broadcast in American history, a record it held for a remarkable twenty-seven years. The 256th episode, a 2½-hour-long movie, was entitled "Good-bye, Farewell and Amen" and was broadcast today in 1983 to 105.97 million viewers. Martinis featured regularly in *M*A*S*H* and Hawkeye famously liked his dry: "I'd like a dry martini, Mr. Quoc, a very dry martini. A very dry, arid, barren, desiccated, veritable dustbowl of a martini. I want a martini that could be declared a disaster area." We're very happy to offer up a Dry Martini to *M*A*S*H* today. This Martini ratio is David Embury's own preferred proportion.

Leap Year Martini

2 shots London dry gin • ½ shot Grand Marnier • ½ shot sweet vermouth • ¼ shot lemon juice

Shake ingredients with ice and strain into chilled glass. Garnish with lemon zest twist.

IT'S A LEAP YEAR!

Don't miss today's Leap Year Martini, created by Harry Craddock for the leap year celebrations at the London Savoy in 1928, as you only get to try it once every four years. The calendar year is based on the astronomical year, but because the astronomical year doesn't repeat in whole days, over time the two fall out of sync. This is corrected by adding a day to the year every four years. It's called a leap year because while a fixed date advances one day of the week from one year to the next, in a leap year it advances by two—it leaps over a day in the week. So if Christmas is on Friday one year it will be on Saturday the next, but if it was a leap year it would jump to Monday.

March

Reality Check

5 fresh raspberries • ⅔ shot vodka • ⅔ shot Becherovka liqueur • ¼ shot fresh lime juice
2¾ shots Pilsner lager • ⅓ shot sugar syrup • 1 dash bitters

Muddle raspberries in base of large shaker. Add ice and other ingredients, then throw four times. Strain into ice-filled glass. Garnish with lime zest twist.

BEER DAY IN ICELAND

Today is Beer Day if you're Icelandic, and it's a day worth celebrating even if you're not. On this day in 1989, after almost seventy-five years of Prohibition, Icelanders were finally allowed to consume beer again. Iceland had partially repealed Prohibition in 1933 (as had the U.S.), primarily because Spain refused to buy Icelandic fish unless Icelanders bought their wines. But beer remained banned for almost three generations after that, and even today Icelanders who want to drink at home have to buy their booze from one of the country's forty-eight state-owned liquor stores. If you love beer, we're sure you'll adore the Reality Check.

Velvet Threesome

¾ shot calvados • ¾ shot Cognac V.S.O.P. • ¾ shot pisco • ½ shot Licor 43 • ¼ shot dry vermouth

Stir ingredients with ice and strain into chilled glass. Garnish with orange zest twist.

LOU WALKS ON THE WILD SIDE

The late, great Lou Reed, one of rock's enduring icons, was born on this day in 1942 in Brooklyn, New York. After an implausible period penning hits for pre-Beatles pop bands and one novelty single, Reed came to fame with the Velvet Underground. The band's lo-fi sound brought them iconic fans including Andy Warhol, who introduced them to husky-voiced actress-model Nico. By the 1970s, Reed was a solo artist, producing *Transformer*, one of the greatest rock albums of all time. He was a man of many talents, like his wife, Laurie Anderson, and friend Patti Smith, and both his lyrics and his photographs have been published in books. We are remembering this complex artist with a Velvet Threesome, a challenging yet accessible harmony of brandies.

Ragtime

½ shot absinthe • 1½ shots rye whiskey • 1 shot Amaro liqueur
1 shot Aperol Aperitivo • 1 dash Peychaud's Bitters

Rinse mixing glass with absinthe. Stir rest of ingredients with ice and strain into chilled glass.
Garnish with orange zest twist.

TIME OUT FOR THE FIRST TIME

The world's largest-circulation weekly newsmagazine, *Time*, celebrates its anniversary today. It was created in 1923, narrowly escaped being called *Facts*, and made its mark thanks to an innovative multimedia campaign that covered both radio and movie theaters, not to mention such cutting-edge topics as "Aeronautics: A Successful Helicopter" and "Aeronautics: A Dreadnaught." *Time* continues to sell today because it covers world news in a concise, accessible way. Its list of the world's most influential people and its picks for Person of the Year—including, over the decades, Hitler, Obama and Mark Zuckerberg—remain news events in their own right. We are wishing *Time* many happy returns with a Ragtime, one of our favorite rye cocktails.

American Breakfast

½ shot maple syrup • 2 shots bourbon whiskey • ½ shot pink grapefruit juice

Shake ingredients with ice and strain into ice-filled glass. Garnish with grapefruit zest twist.

THE U.S. CONSTITUTION BECOMES LAW

The U.S. Constitution is probably America's single most successful export. The first written constitution in world history, it provided a model for more than 160 different countries in its first 200 years of existence, shaping ideas of freedom and citizenship the world over. Comprising fewer than 4,500 words, including its ringing beginning, "We, the people of the United States…," the Constitution remains both the oldest and the shortest written constitution of any government in the world. It entered into law on this day in 1789, and because we think that must have been a great morning for Americans to wake up to, we're celebrating the date with an American Breakfast cocktail.

Cajun Nail

½ shot absinthe
1½ shots Tennessee whiskey
1½ shots Drambuie
3 dashes Peychaud's Bitters
3 dashes bitters

Pour absinthe into ice-filled glass, top with water and leave to stand. Separately stir whiskey, Drambuie and bitters with ice. Discard contents of glass (absinthe, water and ice) and strain stirred drink into empty absinthe-coated glass.

ALL-AMERICAN ABSINTHE DAY

Absinthe has been the drink of choice for artists, poets, writers and painters for a long time now, so having its very own day is long overdue. Yet the Green Fairy was banned in many countries after a moral panic caused the belief that it was absinthe, rather than alcoholism or syphilis, that was sending both Bohemians and ordinary working people mad. It is precisely this ban that makes today Absinthe Day, a holiday most cocktail drinkers will happily adopt: on this day in 1997, the first legal absinthe brand since 1912 went on sale in the U.S. New Orleans sits alongside Paris and Prague in the global trinity of absinthe hotspots, so we feel it's only appropriate to celebrate today with a Cajun Nail, an absinthe-enriched hybrid of the city's iconic Sazerac and that 1930s favorite, the Rusty Nail.

Painkiller

2 shots navy rum
2 shots pineapple juice
1 shot orange juice
1 shot cream of coconut

Blend ingredients with 12 oz. of ice.
Garnish with pineapple wedge.

ASPIRIN APPEARS

Headaches are, we're sad to say, an occupational hazard for the dedicated cocktail lover. So thank goodness for Felix Hoffmann, a genius pharmacist who in one super-productive month invented not only aspirin but heroin, too—and who registered the more savory of his two creations with Berlin's patent office on this day in 1899. Hoffmann extracted the very best of willow bark, a substance some Europeans had used as a pain-killer for millennia, and turned it into a stable medicine. In honor of his discovery, we are drinking a Painkiller, an anesthetizing rum concoction from the British Virgin Islands.

Breakfast Club

1 teaspoon marmalade • 1 teaspoon
runny honey • 2 shots light white rum
1 shot lapsang souchong tea

Stir marmalade and honey with rum until dissolved. Add tea, shake with ice and strain into chilled glass. Garnish with lemon zest.

HAPPY BIRTHDAY, CORNFLAKES

On this day in 1897, Dr. John Kellogg, a Seventh-Day Adventist, served the world's first cornflakes to patients at his Michigan sanitarium, as part of his idea of a healthy diet. But it was his brother William who made them famous, by adding sugar and marketing them as a breakfast food. John sued to stop Will's commercialization of his health product, but he lost, and breakfast has never been the same. We are raising a glass to William Kellogg, and breakfast in general, with a concoction that would have had his brother spinning in his grave, a Breakfast Club.

Pink Lady

2 shots London dry gin • ½ fresh egg
white • ¼ shot pomegranate (grenadine)
syrup • ½ shot lemon juice

Shake ingredients with ice and strain into chilled glass. Garnish with maraschino cherry.

INTERNATIONAL WOMEN'S DAY

International Women's Day was first celebrated today more than a hundred years ago and is now a good reason for a holiday in nations from Zambia to Britain—in Madagascar and Nepal, women actually get the day off. The progress women have made since American socialists first celebrated International Women's Day in 1909 is quite phenomenal: there are female prime ministers and CEOs, while there are only a few countries where women do not have the right to vote. Toast women's rights today with a drink that's both strong and prettily named—the Pink Lady.

American Beauty

2½ shots Cognac V.S.O.P.
½ shot dry vermouth • ½ shot white
crème de menthe • ½ shot orange juice
½ shot pomegranate (grenadine) syrup
¼ shot Shiraz red wine

Shake first five ingredients with ice and strain into chilled glass. Use the back of a soupspoon to float red wine over drink. Garnish with rose petal.

AMERIGO BORN

Born in Florence, Italy, on March 9, 1454, Amerigo Vespucci would go on to give his name to not one but two continents—the Americas. A genius navigator, Vespucci sailed from Europe to South America at least twice, and his letters became bestselling travel literature. Columbus died believing the Americas were in Asia, and Vespucci was the first to recognize that the continents were new to Europeans. Let's toast this citizen of the world, an Italian national who sailed the globe for the Spanish and the Portuguese, with an American Beauty for the beautiful land he discovered.

Bella Donna Daiquiri

1½ shots dark rum
1½ shots amaretto liqueur
½ shot lemon juice
¼ shot sugar syrup • ½ shot cold water

Shake ingredients with ice and strain into chilled glass. Garnish the rim with cinnamon powder.

BELL GIVES WATSON A BELL

Scottish-born inventor Alexander Graham Bell made the world's first telephone call today in 1876 and said, "Mr. Watson, come here! I want to see you." Watson, in the next room, heard Bell's voice down the wire and popped in next door. Seven months later, Bell gave Watson a call from two miles away, and in 1915, he rang Watson from New York, repeating his initial words. Watson, in San Francisco, replied, "It will take me five days to get there now." In honor of Bell, and that first bell, we are enjoying a Bella Donna Daiquiri.

Yellow Belly Martini

1 shot citrus vodka • 1 shot limoncello
liqueur • 1 shot lemon juice
⅛ shot sugar syrup • ½ shot cold water

Shake ingredients with ice and strain into chilled glass. Garnish with lemon zest twist.

BRITAIN'S FIRST DAILY NEWSPAPER

In 1702, in a room above Fleet Street's White Hart pub in London, Edward Mallet launched the *Daily Courant*, England's first regular daily newspaper. A single page divided up into two columns, the *Daily Courant* contained no ads, no gossip, no commentary—just news. Britain may be famous for its tabloid "yellow journalism" today, but Mallet insisted on being objective, since people would have "sense enough to make reflections for themselves." Rather than feeling sour that the *Daily Courant* closed and the yellow press won, why not mix up a Yellow Belly Martini, with limoncello, lemon vodka and lemon juice?

Bishop

7 cloves • 3 shots boiling water • 2 teaspoons runny honey • 2½ shots tawny port • 1 shot orange juice

Use preheated heatproof glass. Muddle cloves in the base of shaker. Add boiling water and stir
in honey and other ingredients. Strain into glass. Dust with grated nutmeg to garnish.

ENGLAND'S FIRST FEMALE PRIEST

In March 1994, Angela Berners-Wilson became the first woman to serve as a Church of England priest, one of thirty-two women ordained on that historic day. From 1975 when the General Synod passed the motion that there were no fundamental objections to the ordination of women yet failed to pass a second motion asking for the legal barriers to be removed, it had been a long, long battle for equal rights. In honor of the Reverend Berners-Wilson, her equally pioneering peers and the first female bishop, we recommend a very old classic cocktail, the Bishop, a splendidly warming combination of port, juice, spices and hot water.

Steep Flight

1 shot calvados • 1 shot vodka • 1 shot Cognac V.S.O.P. • 3 shots apple juice

Shake ingredients with ice and strain into ice-filled glass. Garnish with apple or pear slice.

ROCKETMAN TAKES OFF

Say what you will about the "Human Bullet," F. Rodman Law, he wasn't superstitious. On March 13, 1913, Law made the first known attempt at a manned rocket flight, in a 43-foot craft he designed and built himself. His plan was to launch in Jersey City, ascend about 3,280 feet, then parachute down—a feat even more extraordinary for its time than Felix Baumgartner's Red Bull Stratos of 2012, and considerably more dangerous, as was proved when Law's rocket exploded on launch. Amazingly, he picked himself up from among the fragments, singed and bloody, and walked away. We are lauding Mr. Law, one of the 20th century's unsung heroes, with an aptly named orchard-fruit concoction, the Steep Flight.

Brainstorm

1½ shots bourbon whiskey
¾ shot Bénédictine D.O.M. liqueur
1 shot dry vermouth
½ shot cold water

Stir ingredients with ice and strain.
Garnish with orange zest twist.

EINSTEIN=MC^2

The father of modern physics, Albert Einstein, was born in Ulm, Germany, to Jewish parents, on this day in 1879. Creator of the special theory of relativity, and the world's most superficially simple but intellectually brain-exploding equation, E=MC2, he was also the father of the atom bomb, and would forever regret his decision to become involved in the project. On his death, Einstein's body was cremated, but the pathologist took it upon himself to remove and preserve Einstein's brain for future study. Tests have failed to find any conclusive differences between Einstein's brain and other people's—if anything, it may be slightly smaller — but it still seems appropriate to toast Albert and his cranial mass with a Brainstorm.

The Godfather

2 shots blended scotch whisky • 1 shot amaretto liqueur

Stir ingredients with ice and strain into ice-filled glass. Garnish with a twist of orange.

MOVIE PREMIERE, NEW YORK

On this day in 1972, with padded cheeks and heavy makeup, Marlon Brando stormed on-screen in a movie theater in New York. Three hours later, a cult classic had been born. *The Godfather* is arguably the most famous, and the most quoted, gangster movie of all time, and won Brando an Oscar. But what is a gangster movie without the liquor? With this dark, no-nonsense drink we delve into the criminal underworld and toast the mobster Don Corleone. Only to be enjoyed while wearing a smart tailored suit, preferably black tie, the additional bloodstains are optional. But don't forget, *The Godfather* is a family saga, so feel free to create your own dynasty. Based on vodka instead of whisky, this drink becomes a Godmother. For the more reluctant mobsters among you, do like Michael Corleone and use cognac for a Godchild.

Poet's Dream

1 shot London dry gin • ½ shot Bénédictine D.O.M. liqueur • 1 shot dry vermouth
2 dashes orange bitters • ½ shot cold water

Stir ingredients with ice and strain into chilled glass. Garnish with lemon zest twist.

BOOK SMUGGLER DAY, LITHUANIA

In the days before the Internet, if you wanted information that your government preferred you not to have, books were your only hope—as were book smugglers, such as Jurgis Bielinis, who was born on this very day in 1846 in what is now Lithuania but was then a part of the Russian empire. Despite having only an elementary school education, Bielinis overcame Russia's ban on the Lithuanian language and literature. He smuggled books, newspapers and magazines in both Lithuanian and Latvian, printed his own newspaper and wrote several pamphlets on the history of his nation. Lithuanians commemorate today as Book Smuggler Day, so we are celebrating the freedom of information, and the freedom to choose your own language, with a Poet's Dream.

Shamrock

1½ shots Irish whiskey
1½ shots dry vermouth
½ shot green Chartreuse
½ shot green crème de menthe
½ shot cold water

Shake ingredients with ice and strain into chilled glass.
Garnish with mint.

ST. PATRICK'S DAY

Today is St. Patrick's Day, an excuse for Guinness, nostalgia, wearing green, listening to folk music and generally celebrating the man who, allegedly, banished all snakes from Ireland after they disturbed him while he was fasting. St. Patrick's symbol is the shamrock, which is, most likely, a type of clover. It was a sacred plant to the early Irish Druids because it had three leaves, and the number 3 was sacred in Celtic religion. Sensibly enough, the Christians soon adopted it as a sacred symbol, too. St. Patrick used the shamrock's mystical triad of leaves to teach about Christianity—in particular the Trinity, the holy threesome of Father, Son and Holy Ghost. Should you have a shamrock in hand, do use it to garnish a Shamrock, a garish but very palatable Irish whiskey concoction from Harry Craddock's *The Savoy Cocktail Book*.

Biscotti Spritz

3 shots sparkling wine • 1 shot hazelnut liqueur • 1 shot butterscotch liqueur • top with soda

Pour sparkling wine and liqueurs into glass. Add ice. Top with soda. Serve with biscotti.

FRA ANGELICO, RIP

The folks behind the hazelnut liqueur Frangelico claim that their secret recipe dates back to a hermit monk named Fra Angelico in 18th-century Piedmont, Italy. But the Fra Angelico who died in a Roman monastery on this day in 1455 is rather better attested: one of the true stars of early Italian Renaissance art, this humble, devout monk was known as "Blessed One" during his lifetime, and he would not even pick up a brush without praying first. Today he is beatified—halfway to sainthood—and is the official patron of Catholic artists. We are toasting him with an Italian-inspired cocktail, a take on the northern Italian aperitif Spritz: the Biscotti Spritz includes not only Frangelico but butterscotch, too.

Bridgetown Daiquiri

2 shots golden rum • ½ shot maraschino liqueur • ½ shot sugar syrup
½ shot ruby grapefruit juice • ½ shot lime juice

Shake ingredients with ice and strain into chilled glass. Garnish with red grapefruit wedge.

SYDNEY HARBOUR BRIDGE OPENS

Sydney Harbour Bridge (fondly known as "the Coathanger") opened for public use today in 1932. The opening ceremony didn't run quite as smoothly as planned, though. Just as the guy with the golden scissors was about to cut the ribbon and declare the bridge open, a man on horseback in military uniform galloped past him and slashed the ribbon with his sword. To celebrate the opening, Australians put on some spectacular displays, including a Venetian carnival, marching bands, decorated floats and a procession of passenger ships. Most incredible, though, was the relay of children who carried to the bridge a note written by kids at an elementary school over 320 miles away. Celebrate the iconic bridge's birthday tonight by shaking up a Bridgetown Daiquiri.

Showbiz

1½ shots vodka • ¾ shot crème de cassis
1½ shots pink grapefruit juice

Shake ingredients with ice and strain into chilled glass. Garnish with blackberries.

KING LUDWIG I ABDICATES

The 19th-century Irish courtesan Lola Montez certainly led an impressive life—eloping in her teens, taking up a career as a "Spanish" dancer and dating men ranging from the composer Franz Liszt and the writer Alexandre Dumas to King Ludwig I of Bavaria. As Ludwig's mistress, she wielded considerable power, driving liberal reforms that made both Ludwig and herself unpopular until, on this day in 1848, he abdicated. Lola's career continued to flourish; Ludwig's didn't. We are toasting Lola, and her epic joie de vivre, with a suitably glamorous Showbiz, replete with vodka, cassis and grapefruit.

Twinkle

3 shots vodka • ¾ shot elderflower
liqueur • top with champagne brut

Shake first two ingredients with ice and strain into chilled glass. Top with Champagne. Garnish with lemon zest twist.

WORLD'S FIRST PUBLIC TWEET

On this day in 2006, twenty-nine-year-old Jack Dorsey sent the world's first public Tweet, the remarkably unmemorable "just setting up my twttr," on Twitter, a new service he had founded. Today, Twitter's hundreds of millions of users send more than half a billion Tweets each day—all, of course, at 140 characters or less. Tweets are cited by newspapers as respected as *The Times* of London, while everyone from football players to presidents seems to have an account. Rather than a Tweet, we are indulging in a Twinkle, an elegant elderflower-vodka-champagne blend that like Twitter, has more depth than it at first appears.

Waters of Chaos

1½ shots genever • ¼ shot overproof rum
¼ shot green Chartreuse
¾ shot lime juice • ½ shot sugar syrup
½ shot cold water

Shake ingredients with ice, strain into ice-filled glass. Garnish with lime slice.

WORLD WATER DAY

Water is the most abundant compound on the earth's surface, covering 70 percent of our planet. Yet almost a billion human beings on this planet live without access to clean drinking water, so World Water Day is a day for thought. Encouraging all of us to think about the water we use, organizers state that turning off the tap while you're brushing your teeth, for example, can save more than 2,600 gallons of water a year, and washing fruit in a bowl rather than in running water can save similar amounts. To preserve precious drinking water today, why not try a Waters of Chaos, infused with both overproof rum and Chartreuse?

Japanese Maple

1¾ shots Japanese whisky • ¾ shot lemon juice • ½ shot maple syrup • ½ fresh egg white

Dry shake ingredients. Shake again with ice and strain into chilled glass. Garnish with Angostura mist.

STAR DIRECTOR BORN IN TOKYO

Akira Kurosawa, probably Japan's most influential film director and the man who brought his country's cinema to a global audience, was born in Tokyo on this day in 1910. In a career lasting almost sixty years, he made more than thirty films, including the epic *Seven Samurai* and *Ran*, his adaptation of Shakespeare's *King Lear*. A perfectionist and former painter who both directed and edited his movies, Kurosawa's work inspired George Lucas's vision of the original *Star Wars*, as well as classic Westerns like *The Magnificent Seven* and *A Fistful of Dollars*. Let's remember his legacy with a cocktail based on another great Japanese export: the Japanese Maple, an outstanding Sour-style concoction with Yamazaki whisky.

Dirty Martini

2½ shots London dry gin • ¼ shot olive brine • ¼ shot dry vermouth

Stir ingredients with ice and strain into chilled glass. Garnish with stuffed olive.

THE DAY OF TRUTH AND JUSTICE

Today is a public holiday in Argentina, known as Día de la Memoria por la Verdad y la Justicia, or the Day of Remembrance for Truth and Justice, to commemorate the victims of the Dirty War. It's the anniversary of the coup d'état in 1976 that toppled a government that was fighting anyone to the left of politics. The Dirty War, or Guerra Sucia, was the name used by the Argentine military government for this period of state terrorism against political dissidents. In those days military and security forces clashed with anyone believed to be associated with socialism. The end of the Dirty War seems a good reason to celebrate with a holiday or, if you're not in Argentina, a Dirty Martini.

Little Venice

2 shots sake • 1 shot bourbon whiskey • 1 shot sweet vermouth

Stir ingredients with ice and strain into chilled glass. Garnish with maraschino cherry.

VENICE IS FOUNDED

According to legend, the city of Venice was founded at the stroke of noon on this day in March 421, when the dedication of its first church, San Giacomo di Rialto, is said to have taken place. Nothing of the original church remains today, and the present church on the site is famed for its huge and famously inaccurate, one-handed, 15th-century clock that looms over its Gothic entrance portico. There are no surviving records of the origins of Venice, but some historians believe that its original population was composed of Roman refugees from the nearby undefended countryside and coastline fleeing the Germanic and Hun invasions. Venice is still one of the most beautiful cities in the world, so today we're drinking to its modest origins with a simple but very lovely Little Venice.

Moonlight Cocktail

1½ shots London dry gin • ¼ shot kirschwasser
1 shot sauvignon blanc white wine • 1¼ shots pink grapefruit juice

Shake ingredients with ice and strain into chilled glass. Garnish with lemon zest twist.

WINE TOO LATE FOR BEETHOVEN

A few days before Ludwig van Beethoven died, on this day in 1827, a case of wine arrived from his publisher, prompting the great man's last recorded words: "Pity, pity—too late!" A musical genius, Beethoven started his career as a child piano prodigy, promoted by his overbearing father, and went on to overcome deafness and produce some of the most enduring classical music ever. If you've heard the ringtone tinkle of *Für Elise*, the epic da-da-da-DUM of his Fifth Symphony, or the rippling tones of the *Moonlight Sonata*, you've been influenced by the man. Pay a tribute to his memory not with a sonata but with a Moonlight Cocktail, a delightfully dry blend that includes kirschwasser from his native Germany.

Pulp Fiction

2 shots Cognac V.S.O.P. • 2 shots apple juice • 1 shot apple schnapps liqueur
top with lemon or lime soda

Shake ingredients with ice and strain into ice-filled glass. Top with lemon or lime soda.
Garnish with apple slice.

QUENTIN TARANTINO'S BIRTHDAY

The man who brought us *Pulp Fiction, Reservoir Dogs, Kill Bill, True Romance* and *Django Unchained* celebrates his birthday today. Tarantino is an absolute film geek, an assiduous promoter of smaller movies that might never otherwise have made it to the big screen, and the man who persuaded Brad Pitt to star in *Inglourious Basterds* after an alleged five bottles of wine. We toast the maestro with a Pulp Fiction and wonder why so few of his other movies ever got cocktails named after them. We'd certainly try a True Romance, too.

Elder Aviator

2 shots London dry gin • ½ shot elderflower liqueur • ¼ shot maraschino liqueur
½ shot lemon juice • ½ shot cold water

Shake ingredients with ice and strain into chilled glass. Garnish with lemon zest twist.

SEAPLANE TAKES OFF

As Henri Fabre's Hydravion lifted from the waters of a lagoon outside Marseilles on March 28, 1910, and flew more than 650 yards through the blue French sky, he knew he was making history. His craft, *Le Canard*, a wood-and-canvas monoplane mounted on three floats, had become the first functional seaplane of all time. Fabre would go on to design floats for other seaplane pioneers, yet after World War I he returned to his first love—industrial engineering—with occasional dalliances with inventions. Fabre lived to be 101 years old, an age impressive in anyone, let alone an aviator from those pioneering days. Toast him today with an Elder Aviator, an elderflower twist on the classic Aviation.

London Scramble

2 shots tequila • ½ shot lemon juice • ½ shot lime juice
½ shot agave syrup • ¼ shot crème de mûre

Shake first four ingredients with ice and strain into glass filled with crushed ice. Drizzle créme de mûre over drink (will slowly bleed through the cocktail). Garnish with lemon zest twist and blackberries.

FIRST LONDON MARATHON

According to legend, the original marathon was run in ancient Greece, when a soldier named Pheidippides allegedly raced some twenty-five miles in the high summer heat to deliver the news of victory at the Battle of Marathon. Today, however, marks the anniversary of the first-ever London Marathon in 1981, when, inspired by the New York Marathon, 6,747 nervous runners gathered in the U.K. capital to compete. The race has grown in popularity since then, with competitors age eighteen to over ninety, and a welter of participants in costume raising money for charity by racing as whoopee cushions, camels, giant bananas and more. The London Marathon can be a scramble, so why not celebrate this anniversary with a genuine London Scramble?

Alaskan Martini

2½ shots London dry gin • ¾ shot yellow Chartreuse

Stir all ingredients with ice and strain into chilled glass. Garnish with mint.

AMERICA BUYS ALASKA

On the penultimate day of March 1867, America bought Alaska from Russia for $7.2 million, which works out to roughly two cents per acre. It was bought by U.S. Secretary of State William H. Seward in a deal that was known as "Seward's Folly"—which today doesn't look like such a folly at all. Just to put the numbers into context, the manager of Abu Dhabi's Emirates Palace Hotel spent double that sum on a predecorated Christmas tree. Seward's budget bought America a slice of land twice the size of Texas, which became a genuinely valuable acquisition with the Klondike gold strike just twenty-nine years later. Toast America's forty-ninth state with an Alaskan Martini tonight.

Parisian Spring Punch

1 shot calvados
½ shot dry vermouth
¼ shot lemon juice
¼ shot sugar syrup
top with champagne brut

Shake first four ingredients with ice and strain into ice-filled glass. Top with champagne. Garnish with lemon and lime zest twists.

ET VOILÀ! LA TOUR EIFFEL!

When it officially opened, on this day in March 1899, the Eiffel Tower was the tallest building in the world. It kept that title until New York's Chrysler Building took it away in 1930, though at 108 stories high it's still impressive. The Eiffel Tower was built as the entrance arch to the 1889 World's Fair, which was being held in Paris to mark the centennial celebration of the French Revolution. At the time, there was outrage about the tower—Parisians said it was an eyesore and ruined the skyline. It's now considered to be the most iconic structure in France, attracting more than six million visitors each year. In honor of this landmark, mix up a Parisian Spring Punch this evening. It's a gloriously refreshing and thoroughly Frenchified combo of calvados, citrus and champagne.

April

April Fool

3 shots cold water

Stir with ice and strain into chilled glass.
Garnish with olive.

NATURAL VODKA SPRINGS FORTH IN UKRAINE

It was on this day in 1976 that scientists first analyzed a clear vodka-tasting liquid that was issuing from a spring in southern Ukraine, the grain bowl of the then Soviet Union. Soil analysis of the area suggested that rainwater passing through remnants of grain left on the land over a period of hundreds of years had leached down to levels where ground temperatures were high enough to cause fermentation. As this fermented liquid percolated through ground rock it was clarified, and when it later surfaced as a spring, it was, in fact, a very weak vodka. Locals are believed to have been taking this naturally produced vodka and distilling it to a higher ABV (alcohol by volume) for many years, but the process had been kept as a closely guarded local secret by peasants afraid of losing their natural source of inebriation. Today we're having a laugh and drinking an April Fool....

Baltic Spring Punch

1 fresh peach • 1½ shots rose petal liqueur • ½ shot lemon juice
¼ shot sugar syrup • top with champagne brut

Muddle peach in base of shaker. Add other ingredients, shake with ice and strain into ice-filled glass.
Garnish with peach wedge.

FAIRY TALE KING APPEARS

No childhood would be complete without the stories of Hans Christian Andersen, born today in 1805 in Odense, Denmark. Creator of *The Little Match Girl, The Little Mermaid* and *The Princess and the Pea,* he also wrote *The Snow Queen,* which was the inspiration for Disney's smash hit *Frozen.* Andersen based his story of *The Ugly Duckling* on his own experiences of growing up tall, gawky and just that little bit different. While we remember him for his fairy tales, he wrote poems, plays, novels and travelogues on the side. Let's toast Denmark's most famous son with a Baltic Spring Punch, a floral creation named for the sea by which his country sits, along with, of course, Copenhagen's iconic Little Mermaid statue.

Mudslide

1½ shots Irish cream liqueur • 1½ shots vodka • 1½ shots coffee liqueur • 3 scoops vanilla ice cream

Blend ingredients with two 12 oz. of crushed ice. Garnish with shaved chocolate.

SUNDAE CREATED (ON A SUNDAY)

A classic of the sticky-dessert genre, the ice-cream sundae came into the world on Sunday, April 3, 1892, when a drugstore owner and church treasurer in Ithaca, in upstate New York, treated his minister to a dish of vanilla ice cream tarted up with some cherry syrup and a glacé cherry. Although his subsequent attempts to patent the name "Sunday" proved unsuccessful, the "sundae" name and spelling stuck. Two Rivers, Wisconsin, and Evanston, Illinois, also claim to be the home of the sundae—but Ithaca's cherry Sunday is the only one with documented proof. We are raising a toast to low-rent sweet treats of all varieties with a glass of the gooey, unsophisticated but thoroughly delicious ice-cream cocktail, the Mudslide. Enjoy!

Rat Pack Manhattan

½ shot Grand Marnier • 1½ shots bourbon whiskey • ¾ shot sweet vermouth
¾ shot dry vermouth • 3 dashes bitters

Chill glass, add Grand Marnier, swirl to coat and then discard. Stir other ingredients with ice and strain into liqueur-coated glass. Garnish with orange zest twist and maraschino cherry.

WORLD RAT DAY

Put aside all thoughts of James Herbert's classic horror series, for today is World Rat Day. And no, it isn't sponsored by exterminators, or the World Health Organization for that matter, but by a group of dedicated fans of this once-popular Goth pet. Organizers recommend "bearing gifts and treats to unsuspecting rats," hosting "Ratfests" and generally making "rats very happy." If you don't have a pet rat in hand, we recommend you mark the event with a Rat Pack Manhattan, created in honor of Frank Sinatra's Rat Pack gang of crooners, who sent Vegas wild during their glory days. The Grand Marnier splash that distinguishes the drink represents Sammy Davis Jr., the wild card of the bunch.

Spencer Cocktail

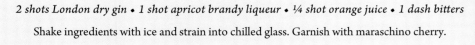

2 shots London dry gin • 1 shot apricot brandy liqueur • ¼ shot orange juice • 1 dash bitters

Shake ingredients with ice and strain into chilled glass. Garnish with maraschino cherry.

TRACY TAKES THE STAGE

Spencer Bonaventure Tracy, one of Hollywood's greatest lead actors, and a man whose naturalistic acting style put him decades ahead of his time, entered the world in Milwaukee, Wisconsin, on this day in 1900. Tracy's work, which he resolutely refused to glamorize, stating that the art of great acting was to "learn your lines," would secure him nine Oscar nominations. The Spencer Cocktail, a mellifluous, fruity harmony of apricot, orange and gin, isn't named for Tracy—it appears in Harry Craddock's 1930 *The Savoy Cocktail Book*, written before Tracy hit the big time. But it does make an excellent tribute to the man who was the love of Katharine Hepburn's life.

Golden Fizz

2 teaspoons runny honey • 1½ shots London dry gin • 1 shot triple sec
1 shot pink grapefruit juice • ¼ shot lemon juice • top with lemon or lime soda

Stir honey with gin in base of shaker until honey dissolves. Add next three ingredients, shake with ice and strain into ice-filled glass. Top with lemon or lime soda. Garnish with orange slice and mint.

OLYMPICS RETURN TO GREECE

More than a hundred years ago today, Athens hosted the 1896 Summer Olympics, the first international Olympics of modern times. The city was the natural choice, given that the games originated in ancient Greece sometime around 776 BC, although these first contemporary Olympics were relatively low-key. The whole affair ran for a mere ten days and included just nine different sports. As at the original ancient Greek Olympics, only men were allowed to compete. Unlike in ancient Greece, they did so fully clothed. Honor champions past, present and future, as well as the first-ever Olympic gold medalist, America's James Connolly, with an aptly named Golden Fizz. A long, gin-based cooler, it's the perfect postworkout refreshment.

Penicillin

3 teaspoons honey water (2:1) • 1½ shots Islay whisky
1 shot blended scotch whisky • ¼ shot ginger liqueur • ¾ shot lemon juice

Shake ingredients with ice and strain into ice-filled chilled glass. Garnish with stem ginger.

WORLD HEALTH DAY

In 1948, shortly after the World Health Organization was established, it designated every April 7 from 1950 onward as World Health Day, to mark the organization's founding—which makes it a perfect opportunity to drink to that miraculous lifesaver, penicillin. Scotland's Sir Alexander Fleming discovered penicillin in 1928, thus transforming modern medicine. The Penicillin cocktail is almost equally miraculous. Created by Australia's Sam Ross during his stint at New York's iconic contemporary speakeasy, Milk and Honey, it's one of the few 21st-century cocktails already acknowledged as a classic. The combination of smoky scotch whisky, fragrant honey, lemon and a hint of ginger tastes better than any medicine—a couple of them will prove almost as magical as antibiotics.

Green Tea Martini

2 shots London dry gin
1 shot Zen green tea liqueur
¼ shot dry vermouth
¾ shot cold green tea

Shake ingredients with ice and strain into chilled glass.
Garnish with mint.

BUDDHA'S BIRTHDAY IN JAPAN

In many parts of Asia, Buddha's birthday is a moveable feast, following a number of different lunar calendars—but the organized Japanese, who use the standard Western calendar, have set April 8 as the date for his birthday, year in, year out. At Hana-Matsuri, or Flower Festival, the Japanese decorate shrines with flowers to commemorate the birth of Siddhartha Gautama, the man who would later become the Buddha, in an orchard of blossoming trees more than 2,000 years ago. Baby Buddhas are placed in the shrines and, to symbolize the nectar with which the original Buddha was sprinkled, worshippers sprinkle the babies with sweet tea. The Green Tea Martini, a subtle, lightly floral gin martini, features both green tea and green tea liqueur. An excellent accompaniment to Japanese desserts at any time of year, it's easily good enough to celebrate Buddha today.

Finnberry Martini

*2 shots vodka • 2 shots cranberry juice
1 shot cloudberry liqueur*

Shake ingredients with ice and fine strain into chilled glass. Garnish with blueberries.

FINNISH LANGUAGE DAY

We have a bishop named Mikael Agricola to thank for the Finnish language. The first person to write the language down, he died on this day in 1557. *"Hei! Tänään on Suomen kieli päivä, aika juhliaihana kirjaimet J ja K sekä lisätä pisteitä niin paljon vokaaleja kuin mahdollista."* Or, as we say in English, "Hello! Today is Finnish Language Day, a time to celebrate the wonderful letters *J* and *K*, and to add dots to as many vowels as possible." The Finnberry Martini, a berry martini starring Finland's signature Lapponia cloudberry liqueur, along with northern cranberries, makes the perfect tribute.

Champino

*1 shot Campari • 1 shot sweet vermouth
top with champagne brut*

Shake first two ingredients with ice and strain into chilled glass. Top with champagne. Garnish with orange zest twist.

THE SAFETY PIN'S BIRTHDAY

One of the world's most prolific inventors, Walter Hunt is credited with an ice plow, bottle-stoppers, road-sweeping machines, a fountain pen, a sewing machine, a repeating rifle, circus equipment and more. On this day in 1849, Hunt picked up a piece of brass wire in his New York City workshop and invented the "Dress-Pin," the little piece of magic we know today as the safety pin. We are toasting Hunt and his thumb-friendly creation with an aptly named Champino, a delectable champagne Negroni. It may have a pin in the name, but it has absolutely no sting in the tail.

Napoleon Market

*2 shots London dry gin • ¼ shot triple sec
• ¼ shot Fernet Branca • ½ shot
Dubonnet Red • ½ shot cold water*

Shake ingredients with ice and strain into chilled glass. Garnish with lemon zest twist.

EXILE EXITS, ELBA-BOUND

Napoleon Bonaparte, the military genius who made his way through the ranks of revolutionary France to eventually crown himself emperor, abdicated and was sent into exile on the island of Elba today in 1814. Napoleon may have given the world the concept of the Napoleon Complex—by which short people make up for their lack of height with aggression—yet at around five feet six inches, Napoleon wasn't especially short for his era. Today's anniversary makes an excellent excuse to discover the splendid Napoleon Market, an elegant, approachable, rust-colored martini that we're sure the great man would have appreciated.

Black Cherry Martini

2½ shots vodka • ¾ shot black raspberry liqueur • ½ shot dry vermouth

Stir ingredients with ice and strain into chilled glass. Garnish with maraschino cherry.

SOCIETY MAG HITS SHELVES

More than three hundred years ago today, the English publisher Richard Steele launched the first version of a society gossip and manners magazine that has been through multiple incarnations but finally settled down as *Tatler*. Steele's version, published under his pen name of Isaac Bickerstaff, Esq., featured gossip from the coffee shops of London and contributors as esteemed as Samuel Johnson. Today's *Tatler* is best known for coverage of socialites and, of course, *The Little Black Book*, its list of London's most eligible under-thirties. Didn't make it into this year's edition of the book? Console yourself with a Black Cherry Martini, a deliciously simple 1990s-style fruit martini.

The Money Penny

*2 shots London dry gin
¾ shot pink grapefruit juice
½ shot dry vermouth
¼ shot sugar syrup
1 dash grapefruit bitters*

Shake ingredients with ice and strain into chilled glass. Garnish with grapefruit zest twist.

HAPPY BIRTHDAY, 007

On this day in 1953, the first book by a onetime British intelligence officer named Ian Fleming rolled off the presses—and James Bond, one of the 20th century's most enduring characters, was born. Despite its then-shocking content of sex and violence, that first edition of *Casino Royale* sold out within a month, though it would not become part of the movie franchise until the 2006 version starring Daniel Craig. Why not toast *Casino Royale*, and Bond and his trusty secretary, by mixing up a delicious gin and grapefruit harmony, The Money Penny?

President

*2 shots light white rum
1 shot orange juice
¼ shot lemon juice
¼ shot pomegranate (grenadine) syrup
½ shot cold water*

Shake ingredients with ice and strain into chilled glass. Garnish with orange zest twist.

MURDER IN THE THEATER

Today is the day on which, in 1865, an actor named John Wilkes Booth shot Abraham Lincoln as he attended the theater. Only twenty-six, Booth was already a stage star. Yet he was also passionately in favor of slavery and passionately against Lincoln, who was wrapping up his successful war against the Confederacy. Even though his life was cut short, Lincoln saved the United States from a permanent split and brought an end to slavery. Let's remember this outstanding president with a President from Harry Craddock's *The Savoy Cocktail Book*.

Flipping Good

2 shots aged rum
½ shot sugar syrup
½ shot whipping cream
1 fresh egg yolk

Dry shake ingredients, then shake again with ice.
Strain into chilled glass. Garnish with grated nutmeg.

GOOD FRIDAY

It may be called Good Friday, Holy Friday, Great Friday or Easter Friday, but whatever it may be called, Good Friday is, of course, the day when Jesus was tried and crucified and then died on the cross, and the veil of the temple in Jerusalem ripped in two. Today in parts of the Philippines, devotees reenact the Crucifixion, flagellating themselves and even undergoing crucifixion; in Guatemala's former capital, Antigua, purple-clad penitents parade through flower-strewn streets as the Semana Santa (Holy Week) celebrations reach their peak. Catholics are supposed to fast today, which means cutting out meat and eating only one full meal and a maximum of two snacks. The Flipping Good cocktail, a contemporary flip enriched with cream and a suitably Eastery egg, is virtually a meal in itself.

Easter Martini

4 cardamom pods
2 shots vanilla vodka
1 shot white crème de cacao liqueur
¼ shot sugar syrup
½ shot cold water
½ fresh egg white

Muddle cardamom pods in base of shaker. Add other ingredients. Shake with ice and strain back into shaker. Dry shake and strain into chilled glass. Garnish with shaved chocolate.

EASTER SUNDAY

Happy Easter! Whether you're celebrating on the Eastern Orthodox calendar or the Western Christian calendar, observing the pagan rites of the spring goddess Eoster or doing nothing religious at all, today is, of course, the day that Christians believe Jesus rose from the dead. Around the world, today is also a day for eating eggs, be they hardboiled and hand-painted like in Lebanon, Poland and Greece, stuffed with confetti as in parts of Mexico and Texas, or crafted from chocolate in the international vein. Whether you are halfway through an epic holiday-weekend party, enjoying a quiet lunch with family, or supervising excited kids at an Easter egg hunt, we recommend serving up an Easter Martini. A classic chocolate martini with hints of vanilla and cardamom, it has a smoothing shot of egg white for an extra-festive touch.

Iced Sake Martini

2 shots vodka • 2 shots sake • ¼ shot ice wine

Stir ingredients with ice and strain into chilled glass. Garnish with cucumber slices.

AND THE BAND PLAYED ON...

Early this morning in 1912, the RMS *Titanic* passenger liner sank beneath the subzero waters of the Atlantic and spiraled almost 13,123 feet down to the silty, pitch-black sea floor. Of all the tales of heroism from that freezing, bitter night, it's the band that stands out. To prevent panic among the hundreds facing certain death, and a potentially lethal storming of the lifeboats, the band stood on the deck and played calming, jaunty tunes. Their bravery and composure, despite knowing they would go down with the ship, most likely saved hundreds of lives. In memory of their heroism, and the iceberg that started it all, we are drinking an Iced Sake Martini, which includes ice wine made from frozen grapes.

Charlie Chaplin Cocktail

¾ shot apricot brandy liqueur • ¾ shot sloe gin • ¾ shot lime juice • ¾ shot cold water

Shake ingredients with ice and strain into chilled glass. Garnish with apricot wedge.

THE LITTLE TRAMP EMERGES

One of film's first superstars, who made his name as the bowler-hatted, cane-wielding Tramp of the silent era, Charles Spencer Chaplin Jr. was born in London today in 1889. He would overcome a brutal childhood, including abandonment, mental illness and stints in a workhouse, to become a star, producer, political activist and father of no fewer than eleven children. Barkeepers at New York City's iconic Waldorf-Astoria created the Charlie Chaplin Cocktail in his honor sometime before 1920, when Chaplin was at the height of his silent-movie fame. Fruity yet bittersweet, it's a splendid tribute to a complex talent. Why not enjoy it with a copy of his masterwork, the 1940 political satire *The Great Dictator*?

Alamagoozlum

1 shot genever • ¾ shot yellow Chartreuse • ¾ shot overproof rum • ¼ shot Grand Marnier
¾ shot sugar syrup • 1 shot cold water • ¼ shot bitters • ¼ fresh egg white

Dry shake ingredients to emulsify. Add ice, shake again and strain into chilled glass.
Garnish with pineapple wedge.

BARTENDING BANKER BORN

In Charles H. Baker's splendidly eccentric 1939 cocktail compendium, *The Gentleman's Companion: Being an Exotic Drinking Book,* he introduces the Alamagoozlum cocktail as "J. Pierpont Morgan's Alamagoozlum: the Personal Mix Credited to that Financier, Philanthropist & Banker of a Bygone Era." The said John Pierpont Morgan, one of the greatest businessmen of America's Gilded Age, was born on this day in 1837. Cocktail author David A. Embury unkindly observed that his creation proves that "as a bartender, he was an excellent banker." We beg to differ. The Alamagoozlum defies its myriad ingredients to deliver a glorious bittersweet mélange of flavors, as well as an insight into the well-stocked wonders of a 19th-century oligarch's home bar. Upgrade your own bar and give one a try tonight.

Aperol Spritz

3 shots Soave wine white • 2 shots Aperol Aperitivo • top with soda

Pour ingredients into ice-filled glass and lightly stir. Garnish with orange wedge.

REAL GAME OF THRONES BEGINS

If you thought the TV series *Game of Thrones* seemed a little over the top, or perhaps even unrealistically grim, allow us to introduce you to the possibly ultimate Renaissance femme fatale, Lucrezia Borgia. Lucrezia came into the world today in Subiaco, near Rome, in 1480, and she makes the incestuous, conniving Cersei from *Game of Thrones* look like quite the pussycat. Daughter of a cardinal who would later become pope, Lucrezia was dogged by rumors of incest with her brother Cesare, who probably had her second husband assassinated, and she scandalously attended Cesare's epic fifty-prostitute orgy, the Banquet of Chestnuts. Besides being the most notorious woman of her era, Lucrezia was a famous patron of the arts. Remember her with an Italian classic, the refreshing Aperol Spritz.

Kopstoot

½ shot genever
½ pint Belgium dubbel beer

Pour genever into shot glass and beer into beer glass.

BELGIUM BECOMES A KINGDOM

For many centuries, Belgium was not a country—it was either a part of an empire or split into smaller, competing states. On this day in 1839, when European powers signed the Treaty of London, it formally moved from being part of the United Kingdom of the Netherlands to nationhood, under the name the Kingdom of Belgium. Today, this little country, with a population of just eleven million, punches well above its weight in beer. Enjoy a Belgian beer in true Belgian style today, as a Kopstoot, traditionally served with a shot of local genever.

Mary Pickford Cocktail

2 shots light white rum
1½ shots pineapple juice
¼ shot pomegranate (grenadine) syrup
⅛ shot maraschino liqueur

Shake ingredients with ice and strain into chilled glass. Garnish with maraschino cherry.

FIRST FILM STAR'S MOVIE DEBUT

Ramón Gómez de la Serra wrote in his 1930 book *Movieland*, "[The Mary Pickford] cocktail produces in one's soul the same effect as the provoking grace of its namesake." The Mary Pickford is a truly international drink, created by Liverpool-born bartender Fred Kaufman in honor of the Canadian–American silent-movie queen at Havana's Hotel Sevilla-Biltmore. Arguably the first-ever film star, and one of the first actors to parlay her success into a production career, Mary Pickford made her screen debut on this day in 1909. It's the perfect excuse to discover this classic, fruity Cuban cocktail from Cuba's golden age.

Roman Punch

1½ shots Bénédictine D.O.M. liqueur
1½ shots Cognac V.S.O.P. • *¾ shot overproof rum* • *¾ shot lemon juice*

Shake ingredients with ice and strain into glass filled with crushed ice. Stir and top ice if necessary. Garnish with lemon slice.

ROMULUS FOUNDS HIS CITY

Romulus and Remus, the legendary brothers who founded Rome, did not have the best start in life. Despite the fact that they were the sons of the war god, Mars, their mother was forced to abandon them as infants. They were suckled by a she-wolf and then raised by a shepherd. On this day in 753 BC, or so the story goes, the twins returned as adults to found a new city, which Romulus would christen Rome after himself, having killed his sibling in a vicious town-planning dispute. We're marking the anniversary of this fabulous city with a potent, refreshing Roman Punch.

Green Swizzle

2 shots light white rum
¼ shot white crème de menthe
½ shot lime juice
¼ shot sugar syrup • 1 dash bitters

Pour ingredients into glass. Fill glass with crushed ice and stir.

GO GREEN FOR EARTH DAY

Earth Day is probably the biggest event on the green calendar. More than a billion people, in 190 countries, take part each year. It's easy to perform one green act today: take the bike instead of the car, plant a tree, switch your lightbulbs over to sustainable ones, or volunteer to clean up your community. Once you're done, reward yourself with a suitably green cocktail, the Green Swizzle. This lightly minty Daiquiri-style affair was a Trinidadian specialty as far back as the 1920s, when P. G. Wodehouse's Bertie Wooster enjoyed several at a Planter's Bar.

English Martini

1 sprig rosemary
2½ shots London dry gin
1 shot elderflower liqueur

Strip rosemary leaves from stem and muddle in base of shaker. Add other ingredients, shake with ice and strain into chilled glass. Garnish with rosemary sprig.

ST. GEORGE'S DAY

St. George is the patron saint of England and gives his name to the English flag, the St. George's Cross, a red cross on a white background. Yet George was actually quite an international character. Born in Syria, he was a Roman soldier and killed his famous dragon in Libya. With all due respect to Beirutis, Catalans and, of course, Georgians, who also consider George a patron, we are marking his saint's day with a thoroughly English cocktail, the English Martini. It's a spring-fresh marriage of London dry gin, elderflower and rosemary.

Atomic Dog

1½ shots light white rum
¾ shot melon liqueur
¾ shot coconut rum liqueur
2½ shots pineapple juice
¾ shot lemon juice

Shake ingredients with ice, strain into ice-filled glass. Garnish with pineapple wedge and maraschino cherry.

DUPLICATE DOG DEBUTS

Happy Birthday, Snuppy! And, yes that is Snuppy, not Snoopy. The world's first cloned dog was conceived in South Korea by a team of scientists using skin cells from a black Afghan hound named Tai. Since his birth, on this day in 2005, Snuppy has become a father himself, by artificially inseminating two female clones. More bizarrely, a set of cloned sniffer dogs, all named Toppy, now help patrol South Korea's airports. Let's drink to all these dogs today with a bright green Atomic Dog.

Espresso Martini

1½ shots vodka • 1½ shots espresso • ½ shot coffee liqueur • ¼ shot sugar syrup

Shake ingredients with ice and strain into chilled glass. Garnish with coffee beans.

ANZAC DAY

Since 1916, both Australia and New Zealand have commemorated today as Anzac (the Australian and New Zealand Army Corps) Day, a chance to remember the men and women who lost their lives fighting for the empire. On April 25, 1915, the first Australian and New Zealand Army Corps forces landed at Gallipoli, marking the start of the Gallipoli campaign. Though other forces fought in the campaign, Gallipoli is part of the heritage of three nations: it was a defining step in the journey to independence for both Australia and New Zealand, and a career triumph for Mustafa Kemal Atatürk, who went on to found modern Turkey. At military services, soldiers begin commemorations with a "gunfire breakfast" of coffee and rum, the substance that fueled Anzac forces at Gallipoli. Dick Bradsell's iconic Espresso Martini makes an extremely palatable substitute.

Merchant of Venice

2 teaspoons runny honey • 2 shots vodka • ½ shot Aperol Aperitivo
½ shot lemon juice • ½ fresh egg white

Stir honey with vodka in base of shaker to dissolve. Add other ingredients and dry shake.
Shake again with ice and strain into chilled glass. Garnish with lemon zest twist.

BARD BAPTIZED

There is not a lot known about the life of the world's greatest playwright except his work: most scholars believe that Shakespeare produced as many as 37 plays in his short life, as well as more than 150 poems. Although many people commemorate his birthday on St. George's Day (April 23), his actual date of birth isn't known for certain—we only know that he was baptized on today's date in 1564, in Stratford-upon-Avon, England. To honor the man who started as a freelance actor and became a titan of literary history, we have chosen a smooth and elegant Aperol-based concoction, the Merchant of Venice, named for one of his plays.

King of Orange

1½ shots vodka
¾ shot Grand Marnier
½ shot Campari
½ shot lemon juice

Shake ingredients with ice and strain into chilled glass.
Garnish with orange zest twist to resemble a crown.

IT'S KING'S DAY IN THE NETHERLANDS

You can't fail to notice that orange is the national color of the Netherlands and the ruling House of Orange-Nassau on April 27. Today the entire country turns orange to celebrate King's Day, the birthday of King Willem-Alexander. A tradition since 1890, the day changed from Queen's Day in 2013 when Queen Beatrix abdicated and the first king since the national holiday was established ascended the throne. Orange madness takes over and everyone lets their hair down (often dyed orange) and dresses up in extravagant orange outfits. And for just this one day goods can be sold on the street without a permit, so lots of people put tables outside their houses piled with their unwanted goods as part of a nationwide flea market. We're toasting the king and the Netherlands with a King of Orange.

Tequila Mockingbird

2 shots tequila
½ shot green crème de menthe
½ shot lime juice
⅛ shot sugar syrup

Shake ingredients with ice and strain into chilled glass.
Garnish with mint.

HARPER LEE'S BIRTHDAY

For fifty-five years *To Kill a Mockingbird* was the only novel published by Nelle Harper Lee, who was born on this day in 1926. Then to the amazement of the world, it was announced in 2015 that *Go Set a Watchman*, the novel she wrote prior to *Mockingbird*, would be published. Although written before the gently autobiographical *Mockingbird*, which is both a coming-of-age story and a depiction of racial prejudices in the South, *Go Set a Watchman* features the same characters in later life. *Mockingbird* won the Pulitzer Prize for Fiction in 1961, and the following year the film version won four Academy Awards, including Best Actor for Gregory Peck. Named for Harper Lee's book, the Tequila Mockingbird cocktail is thought to have been created in the 1960s.

The Bird Is the Word

1½ shots tequila • 1 shot yellow Chartreuse • ½ shot apricot brandy liqueur • 1 shot lemon juice

Shake ingredients with ice and strain into chilled glass. Garnish with lemon zest twist.

BIRTH OF THE THESAURUS

A British physician named Peter Mark Roget signed off on the preface to the first thesaurus of the modern era today in 1852, his compendium of synonyms saving the day for writers and crossword-puzzle fans ever since. An obsessive-compulsive workaholic and list maker, Roget started work on his masterpiece in 1805 and would put it through twenty-eight more editions before his death in 1869. If you, like us, have ever struggled for the right word, *Roget's Thesaurus* is one innovation that deserves appreciation. Why not do so with The Bird Is the Word? This grappa-based take on the Prohibition-era cocktail known as The Last Word showcases the herbal notes of green Chartreuse.

Orange Brûlée

1½ shots amaretto liqueur • 1½ shots Grand Marnier • ¾ shot Cognac V.S.O.P. • ¼ shot whipping cream

Shake first three ingredients with ice and strain into chilled glass. Float thin layer of cream over drink and turn glass to spread evenly. Garnish with cocoa powder.

BICYCLING QUEEN STEPS DOWN

A msterdam saw its last Queen's Day for the foreseeable future on this day in 2013, when Queen Beatrix, the seventy-five-year-old monarch, formally abdicated and handed the reins of state to her son, Willem-Alexander. Willem-Alexander is the Netherlands' first king since 1890, Beatrix is now Princess Beatrix, and Amsterdam celebrates King's Day around his birthday on April 27. Both belong, of course, to the House of Orange, which is why Amsterdam marks its royal days with orange installations, orange clothes, orange food and orange drinks. We are honoring Princess Beatrix and her bicycle-riding son with an Orange Brûlée, a regally luscious after-dinner drink enriched with orange, almond, cognac and a decadent cream float.

May

Floral Martini

2 shots London dry gin
½ shot elderflower liqueur
½ shot dry vermouth
¼ shot rose water
½ shot cold water

Stir ingredients with ice and strain into chilled glass.
Garnish with rose petal.

MAY DAY

The ancient pagan festival of May Day is celebrated throughout the northern hemisphere, but it is particularly big in Germany, where it's a national holiday. May Day is all about welcoming the spring, chasing away evil spirits and, in Germany, feeling relief that Witches' Night, or Walpurgisnacht, is over. In towns everywhere, the community turns out in the square for the ceremonial raising of the maypole (Maibaum) and the festivities that follow, with traditional music, dances and, of course, beer and sausage. The earliest May Day celebrations can be traced back to the Floralia, or festival of Flora, which was held to worship the Roman goddess of flowers, and that's why today we will be lightheartedly drinking a Floral Martini.

Polish Martini

¾ shot vodka
¾ shot bison grass vodka
¾ shot spiced honey liqueur
¾ shot apple juice

Shake ingredients with ice and strain into chilled glass.
Garnish with apple slice.

FLAG DAY IN POLAND

A country that has suffered so much loss of independence during its tumultuous history takes its flag day seriously. Partitioned in 1772 between Prussia, Russia and Austria, then in 1793 between Russia and Prussia, and then in 1795 it ceased to exist as a nation-state for 123 years and only regained independence in 1918. But within months the newly established Second Republic of Poland again had to defeat a predatory Russia. Then in September 1939 it was attacked by Germany from the west and a couple of weeks later by Russia from the east, and suffered its fourth partition. Hitler and Stalin's objective was to eradicate Polish culture—everything from playing Polish music to flying the Polish flag. After World War II ended, Poland remained behind the Iron Curtain for more than four decades. However, with the growth of the Solidarity movement under Lech Walesa and with the spiritual help of the Polish-born Pope John Paul II, it broke free. Today starts a three-day celebration that also takes in International Workers' Day on May 1 and Constitution Day on May 3. Today we drink to Poland's freedom with a Polish Martini.

The Journalist

2 shots London dry gin • ¼ shot triple sec • ½ shot dry vermouth • ½ shot sweet vermouth
¼ shot lemon juice • 2 dashes bitters

Shake ingredients with ice and strain into chilled glass. Garnish with maraschino cherry.

WORLD PRESS FREEDOM DAY

This day was established by the United Nations General Assembly (UNESCO) to maintain awareness of the importance of freedom of the press and to remind governments of their duty to respect and uphold the right to freedom of expression. It was also to mark the anniversary of the Declaration of Windhoek, a statement of free-press principles put together by African newspaper journalists in 1991. Today UNESCO will confer its Guillermo Cano World Press Freedom Prize to an individual, organization or institution that has made an outstanding contribution to the defense and/or promotion of press freedom. The prize is named for Guillermo Cano Isaza, a Colombian journalist who was assassinated by drug barons in Bogotá on December 17, 1986. How else to remember him today than with a Journalist cocktail?

Darth Jäger

1 shot Jägermeister • 3 shots medium dry cider

Pour Jägermeister into shot glass. Place old-fashioned glass over shot glass and upend to leave full shot glass now upside-down in old-fashioned glass. Slowly pour cider into old-fashioned glass.

STAR WARS DAY

May the fourth be with you! Around the world *Star Wars* fans are celebrating *Star Wars* Day today. It's a completely random date and is believed to have originated on May 4, 1979, the day on which Margaret Thatcher took office as British prime minister. An advertisement in the *London Evening News* read "May the Fourth Be with You, Maggie. Congratulations." The Los Angeles city council, however, chooses to celebrate *Star Wars* Day on May 25, the anniversary of the release of the first film in the *Star Wars* series. If you're choosing to celebrate today, we're proposing a drink that's just a bit more sophisticated than those served in the Chalmun's Cantina, the famous *Star Wars* bar on the planet of Tattooine, and it's a Darth Jäger.

Mexican 55

1½ shots tequila • 1 shot lemon juice • ½ shot sugar syrup
2 dashes bitters • top with champagne brut

Shake first four ingredients with ice and strain into ice-filled glass. Top with champagne.
Garnish with lime wedge.

CINCO DE MAYO

Cinco de Mayo, or Fifth of May, is one of those peculiar celebrations that are honored more outside their homelands than within. The day commemorates the victory of the Mexican army over invading French forces at the battle of Puebla on May 5, 1862. In that same year, Mexican-Americans fighting in the Civil War took on the battle of Puebla and its date as a symbol of pride. Mexican-American communities all over the U.S. will be partying hard today and what better way to celebrate than with a Mexican 55, an adaptation of the classic French 75 created in 1988 at La Perla, Paris, France. The name comes from Fidel Castro's statement that bullets, like wine, came in vintages and Mexican 55 was a good year [for bullets].

Three Miler

1½ shots Cognac V.S.O.P. • 1½ shots light white rum
½ shot pomegranate (grenadine) syrup • ½ shot lemon juice

Shake ingredients with ice and strain into chilled glass. Garnish with lemon zest twist.

THE UNDER FOUR-MINUTE MILE

Today in 1954 Sir Roger Bannister set a world record for the mile and also became the first man to run the mile in under four minutes, covering the distance on a slow track with difficult crosswinds in 3 minutes 59.4 seconds, and he wasn't even a professional athlete; he was a medical student. He trained during his lunch breaks and on weekends—and went to work on the morning he ran the record-breaking mile. Without nutritionists, sports psychologists or intensive training, he ran faster than any man had ever run before. He then hung up his custom-made running shoes and built a career as a pioneering neurologist, an academic and a president of the Sports Council of Great Britain. Today we're drinking to Bannister's achievement with a Three Miler.

Perfect Lady

2 shots London dry gin
¾ shot lemon juice
¾ shot green crème de peche (peach) liqueur
½ shot egg white

Shake ingredients with ice and fine strain into chilled glass. Garnish with peach slice.

MOTHER'S DAY

Very wisely, the world has been worshipping mothers for thousands of years. The day was first celebrated in its modern guise in the United States when Anna Jarvis held a memorial for her mother in West Virginia in 1908 and began a campaign to make "Mother's Day" a recognized holiday. In 1914 President Woodrow Wilson signed a proclamation declaring the second Sunday in May to be Mother's Day and a national holiday. As the celebration spread globally, its date was changed to fall in line with similar events, often linked to the majority religion, such as Virgin Mary Day in Catholic countries. In England it corresponded to Mothering Sunday, which was a traditional celebration of the mother church held on the fourth day of Lent, when child workers were allowed to go home. Some countries selected a date with historical significance. In Bolivia, Mother's Day is on May 27 because on that date in 1812 Spanish troops slaughtered hundreds of local women fighting for independence in the battle of La Coronilla. Even if you are not with your mother on Mother's Day, why not raise a toast to her with a Perfect Lady?

Fallen Angel

2 shots London dry gin
1 shot lemon juice
¼ shot green crème de menthe
¼ shot sugar syrup

Shake ingredients with ice and strain into chilled glass. Garnish with mint.

EARTHQUAKE IN ISTANBUL

If you've ever visited Istanbul's monumental Hagia Sophia, you may have wondered how its extraordinary dome stays up. Well, it hasn't always, because on this day in 558 it collapsed during an earthquake. Legend has it that Emperor Justinian was inspired to build the dome following a visitation by an angel in a dream. It was to be higher and wider than any previously built, and held aloft with a minimum of support to create the illusion of floating. Today we're drinking a Fallen Angel as we think about poor Justinian standing amid the rubble of his angel-inspired dome.

Red Angel

2 shots Shiraz red wine • 1 shot Grand Marnier • ¼ shot maraschino liqueur
½ shot cold water

Stir ingredients with ice and strain into chilled glass. Garnish with orange zest twist.

RED CROSS AND RED CRESCENT DAY

Before Henry Dunant created the Red Cross in 1863, there was no agreement on treating battlefield casualties—wounded were picked up by colleagues under fire unless a truce had been negotiated. We have the Red Cross to thank for the first-ever Geneva Convention, which, in 1864, began to define what was acceptable and unacceptable in times of war. Its medics, who operate as the Red Crescent in Islamic countries, still provide assistance in times of conflict around the world. Today is Henry Dunant's birthday, and Red Cross Day as well—we think they both deserve a toast with a Red Angel.

Russian Spring Punch

7 fresh raspberries • 1½ shots vodka
¼ shot crème de framboise liqueur
¼ shot crème de cassis • ¾ shot lemon juice • ¼ shot sugar syrup
top with champagne brut

Shake first six ingredients with ice and strain into glass filled with crushed ice. Top with champagne; lightly stir. Garnish with berries.

VICTORY DAY IN RUSSIA

In the presence of the brilliant General Georgy Zhukov, on this day in 1945 on Moscow time, the Soviet Union accepted the surrender of the German army. The Russians, who suffered incredibly high losses of between twenty-five and thirty million Soviet citizens, call World War II the Great Patriotic War. This anniversary is still very important to many Russians, who will be marking today with parades, celebrations and fireworks—not to mention, of course, a healthy (or unhealthy) consumption of vodka. What else to drink on a day like today but a vodka-based and champagne-topped Russian Spring Punch?

Mr. President

1¼ shots light white rum
¾ shot sweet vermouth
½ shot Campari.

Stir ingredients with ice and strain into chilled glass.
Garnish with orange zest twist.

NELSON MANDELA BECOMES PRESIDENT OF SOUTH AFRICA

On this day in 1994 Nelson Mandela became South Africa's first black president, sounding the death knell to the era of apartheid, a time when citizens of South Africa were separated in work, life and play because of the color of their skin. Many of the black majority were crammed into ghettoes, and white supremacy was assumed. The guiding light for people of all races, and a Nobel Peace Prize winner, Mandela served a total of twenty-seven years in prison for his fight for freedom, eighteen of them on the notorious Robben Island. Today we are sadly missing Nelson Mandela, who died in 2013, so we will drink to his extraordinary life with a Mr. President.

Moondream

3 shots London dry gin • 1 shot Manzanilla sherry • ¼ shot dry vermouth • ¼ shot crème de pêche

Stir ingredients with ice and strain into chilled glass. Garnish with peach slice.

SALVADOR DALÍ CRACKS THE EGG

Few painters have created more iconic images and been more of an iconic image themselves than the Spanish painter Salvador Dalí, born today in 1904. Dalí was a leader of the Surrealist movement, but being apolitical, as World War II approached, he clashed with the group, and he was expelled during a trial in 1934. In fact, Surrealism was just one phase in the life of this eccentric man, and he moved on to what is known as his classical period. Dalí's lovingly created works carry an incredible tenderness for the human condition. He left behind a monumental volume of work in a wide range of media, from oil paintings to sculpture, furniture, films, photography, ballet costumes, scenery and jewelry. If only Dalí could join us for today's cocktail in his memory, a Moondream.

Limerick

2 shots Irish whiskey • 1 shot lime juice • ½ shot sugar syrup • top with soda

Shake first three ingredients with ice and strain into ice-filled glass. Top with soda water and lightly stir. Garnish with lime wedge.

LIMERICK DAY

Limerick Day celebrates the birth on this day in 1812 of Edward Lear, who popularized the limerick in his 1846 *Book of Nonsense*. He didn't invent the form, which had been around since the early 18th century, but he made it readily available and fun, so today we're toasting Mr. Lear with one of our own creations, a Limerick. Oh, and here's a very bad limerick penned in our office: There was a young bartending star/Who dreamed he would open a bar/Then he worked for a brand/Took a corporate stand/And ended up doing PR.

Bellini

2 shots peach purée
½ shot crème de pêche
¼ shot lemon juice
top with sparkling wine

Shake first three ingredients with ice and strain into chilled glass. Add sparkling wine and gently stir. Garnish with peach slice.

HARRY'S BAR OPENS IN VENICE

Quite a few celebrated barflies have passed through Harry's Bar in its time: Ernest Hemingway, F. Scott Fitzgerald, Dorothy Parker and more. With its very quirky and rather strict, old-fashioned service, Harry's continues as a place of pilgrimage for cocktail enthusiasts passing through Venice. Opened on this day in 1931 by Giuseppe Cipriani, Harry's is the home of one of the most famous cocktails of all time, the Bellini, and that's why we'll be drinking that famous drink today.

Sunshine Cocktail

1½ shots light white rum
1½ shots dry vermouth
1½ shots pineapple juice
⅛ shot pomegranate (grenadine) syrup

Shake ingredients with ice and strain into chilled glass. Garnish with pineapple wedge.

LOUIS XIV CROWNED KING OF FRANCE

Crowned on this day in 1643 at the young age of just four, Louis XIV of France built the Palace of Versailles, established France as one of the preeminent powers of Europe, outlawed Protestants and reigned for seventy-two years and 110 days—which remains the record for the longest reign in a major European country. Louis chose the sun as his emblem and was known as the Sun King, so what else to toast him with but a Sunshine Cocktail?

Death by Chocolate

1 shot vodka
1½ shots Irish cream liqueur
1 shot dark crème de cacao liqueur
3 scoops chocolate ice cream

Blend ingredients with 1 lb. 8 oz. of crushed ice. Garnish with chocolate shavings.

NATIONAL CHOCOLATE CHIP DAY

Someone, somewhere, quite randomly we're sure, decided that today is National Chocolate Chip Day. We're not going to research the veracity of the day too closely because we don't want to blow this opportunity to raid the freezer for the chocolate ice cream and drink a completely guilt-free Death by Chocolate.

I B Damm'd

2 shots genever • ½ shot elderflower liqueur • ¼ shot peach schnapps liqueur • 1¾ shots apple juice

Shake ingredients with ice and strain into chilled glass. Garnish with peach wedge.

DAM BUSTERS!

Operation Chastise began on the evening of this day in 1943 when a British Royal Air Force squadron set out for the Ruhr valley. The aim was to destroy three German dams using clever "bouncing bombs," and therefore flood Germany's industrial heartland. More than a third of the 133 men who took part in the raid died on that night, but two large dams were successfully destroyed. The squadron leader, Guy Gibson, would be awarded the Victoria Cross and go on a public relations tour of the U.S. and Canada. Although immortalized in the brilliant 1955 movie *The Dam Busters*, in real life Gibson was not so fortunate, as sadly he was killed in 1944. Tonight we're toasting all those brave men with an I B Damm'd.

Northern Lights

1½ shots bison grass vodka • ¾ shot apple schnapps liqueur • ½ shot Pernod
1 shot apple juice • ½ shot lime juice • ½ shot sugar syrup

Shake ingredients with ice and strain into chilled glass. Garnish with star anise.

NORWAY'S CONSTITUTION DAY

The constitution of Norway, which declared the country to be an independent nation, was signed on this day in 1814. Although full independence was achieved only in 1905, Norwegians celebrate their nationhood today. Many Norwegians will wear their colorful regional costume, or *bunad*, consisting of finely tailored suits and elaborate milkmaid-styled costumes. Tens of thousands of people will turn out to watch long parades of schoolchildren and local marching bands, many of them starting as early as 7 AM. Our celebration will be to drink a Northern Lights cocktail, named for the Aurora Borealis, that incredible light display of charged particles in the sky, which can be seen over northern Norway on clear, dark winter nights.

Monte Cassino

¾ shot rye whiskey
¾ shot Bénédictine D.O.M. liqueur
¾ shot yellow Chartreuse
¾ shot lemon juice
½ shot cold water

Shake ingredients with ice and strain into chilled glass. Garnish with lemon zest twist.

MONTE CASSINO IS TAKEN

The Polish flag is flying over the ruins of the ancient Italian monastery which has been a symbol of German resistance since the beginning of the year." So ran the news on this day in 1944. The World War II battle of Monte Cassino had lasted four months and was a critical conflict in the Allied advance north through Italy. Today, we're drinking a Monte Cassino to remember all the lives that were lost in that notoriously hideous struggle.

Jackie O's Rose

2 shots light white rum
½ shot triple sec
1 shot lime juice
½ shot sugar syrup
½ teaspoon rose water

Shake ingredients with ice and strain into chilled glass. Garnish with lime wedge.

IN MEMORY OF JACQUELINE KENNEDY ONASSIS

One of Jacqueline Kennedy's first acts as First Lady was to replace the tradition of punch before dinner with cocktails—and to install bars in the White House. Brilliant, educated and beautiful, Jacqueline could set a fashion trend just by wearing an item— and tragedy made her iconic. Although famously discreet, she is rumored to have dallied with some impressive men, among them Frank Sinatra and Marlon Brando. We're toasting Jackie, who died today in 1994, with a Jackie O's Rose.

Blue Passion

1 shot light white rum
1 shot blue curaçao liqueur
1¾ shots lime juice
1 shot sugar syrup

Shake ingredients with ice and strain into glass filled with crushed ice. Garnish with orange zest twist.

LEVI'S BIRTHDAY

Fashion history was made today in 1873 when Levi Strauss and his business partner, Jacob Davis, received a patent giving them exclusive rights to strengthen workingmen's pants with metal rivets. The rivet was created in response to a customer who kept ripping the pockets of his pants, thus transforming hard-wearing denim pants, which had been around for years, into the items we know today as jeans. We're betting that at some point in your life you've had a pair of jeans you adored, so why not remember them today with a Blue Passion?

Caribbean Breeze

1¼ shots light white rum • ½ shot crème de banane liqueur • 2½ shots pineapple juice • 2 shots cranberry juice ½ shot lime cordial

Shake ingredients with ice and strain into ice-filled glass. Garnish with pineapple wedge.

AFRO-COLOMBIAN DAY

Día de la Afrocolombianidad commemorates the 1851 abolition of slavery in Colombia and highlights the artistic, intellectual and social contributions of Afro–Colombians in Colombia. The day also marks the 17th-century founding of the first village of free slaves in South America, Palenque de San Basilio, which is the only such village that survives today, and its inhabitants very much live by traditional African customs. They are also lucky enough to live on the Caribbean coast, so today we're drinking a Caribbean Breeze and wishing we were there to join in on the colorful celebrations.

Black Cocktail

7 fresh blackberries • ½ shot Pernod 1½ shots vodka • ½ shot crème de mûre 1 shot lime juice • ⅛ shot vanilla sugar syrup • ¾ shot cold water

Shake ingredients with ice and strain into chilled glass. Garnish with blackberries.

WORLD GOTH DAY

Around the world today, thousands of black-clad nihilists will be upping the makeup, and partying like it's 1985. You can join them in some quite surprising places, including Attiki, Mexico City, Cape Town, Madrid, Puebla, São Paulo—even Winnipeg!—as well as more obvious spots like Berlin, London and San Francisco. Goth culture originated in England during the early 1980s as an offshoot of punk. Where other trends have faded away, it has continued to grow and evolve, taking its imagery and references from 19th-century Gothic literature and contemporary horror films. If you want to join all those moody souls, just for one day, no drink is darker than a Black Cocktail.

Bitter Lady

1½ shots London dry gin • 1 teaspoon runny honey • ¼ shot Campari • ½ shot lemon juice • ½ fresh egg white

Shake ingredients with ice and strain into chilled glass. Garnish with grapefruit zest twist.

GOOD-BYE TO CATHERINE OF ARAGON

Henry VIII: Renaissance man; lover of wine, women, song and jousting; poet and musician with the bad habit of ditching wives and breaking up churches. It began to go wrong on this day in 1533 when he got rid of Catherine of Aragon by having his marriage to her annulled. How must she have felt, knowing that by then he'd already been married to Anne Boleyn for four months? But then how must Anne Boleyn have felt when she was beheaded for treason three years later? And all Henry wanted was a son. Despite working his way through six wives, he achieved just one male heir, who died at age fifteen. For all the poor women who crossed Henry's path, today we'll be drinking a Bitter Lady.

Ritz Cocktail

¾ shot Cognac V.S.O.P. • *½ shot triple sec* • *¼ shot maraschino liqueur*
¼ shot lemon juice • *top with champagne brut*

Stir first four ingredients with ice and strain into chilled glass. Top with champagne.
Garnish with orange zest twist.

BIRTHDAY OF THE RITZ, LONDON

Today in 1906 the legendary hotelier César Ritz opened the London Ritz, not far from the Savoy, from which he had been fired less than a decade earlier after thousands of pounds' worth of booze mysteriously disappeared. The thirteenth son of a Swiss farmer, Ritz started as a waiter in a small hotel, whose owner told him he would never succeed in his dream of becoming a hotelier. Ritz moved to Paris at the age of seventeen, and just over two decades later he had started a restaurant with the chef Auguste Escoffier and had managed the Savoy. He then opened the Ritz Paris, still one of the great hotels of the world, and the Ritz London came eight years later. So today why not toast the London Ritz with a Ritz Cocktail, created by master mixologist Dale DeGroff?

Earl Grey Fizz

1 shot vodka • *½ shot cold Earl Grey tea* • *¼ shot sugar syrup* • *top with champagne brut*

Shake first three ingredients with ice and strain into chilled glass. Top with champagne.
Garnish with lemon zest twist.

TOWEL DAY

Fans of the late, great Douglas Adams, creator of *The Hitchhiker's Guide to the Galaxy*, will today be celebrating his work. And they do this by carrying towels because, as h2g2 geeks know, "A towel is about the most massively useful thing an interstellar hitchhiker can have." Adams's antihero, Arthur Dent, goes to extreme lengths to get a cup of tea—Earl Grey, to be precise. And so we are marking today with an Earl Grey Fizz.

Kangaroo Dry Martini

2 shots vodka • ½ shot dry vermouth

Stir ingredients with ice and strain into chilled glass. Garnish with lemon zest twist.

NATIONAL SORRY DAY

Since 1998 National Sorry Day has been held in Australia on this date, as a nationwide apology to the Stolen Generations, and on May 26, 2008, Kevin Rudd, then prime minister of Australia, delivered a formal apology to Indigenous Australians. From the late 1800s to as recently as the 1970s, mixed-race Aboriginal children were removed from their families and forcibly placed into institutions or adopted. Many would never see their families again. The purpose was to "civilize" them by removing them from their own language and culture. Today on National Sorry Day, we are remembering, but also saying good-bye to, a difficult past, with a drink bearing the name of one of Australia's most famous symbols, a Kangaroo Dry Martini.

Jol'tini

1¾ shots vanilla-infused vodka • ½ shot coffee liqueur
1¼ shots espresso coffee • ¼ shot vanilla sugar syrup

Shake ingredients with ice and strain into chilled glass. Garnish with coffee beans.

ANGELINA JOLIE/BILLY BOB THORNTON DIVORCE

These two Hollywood stellars were married for just three years before divorcing on this day in 2003. Jolie was Billy Bob's fifth wife, so it's probably not surprising that even wearing vials of each other's blood around their necks couldn't keep them together. Apparently the end came because he didn't want kids and, as we all know, she wanted lots. Anyway, it's all just a great excuse to drink the marvelously named cocktail, a Jol'tini—a nice play on jilted and jolted and Jolie, we think!

Vesper Dry Martini

2 shots London dry gin • ⅔ shot vodka • ⅓ shot Lillet Blanc

Shake ingredients with ice and strain into chilled glass. Garnish with lemon zest twist.

IAN FLEMING'S BIRTHDAY

The creator of James Bond, Ian Fleming worked in British naval intelligence during World War II, and his wartime experience of running a crack unit of specialized intelligence commandoes contributed hugely to his James Bond novels. Both during the war and after it, as a newspaper foreign editor he drank gin pretty much by the gallon. He published his first Bond novel, *Casino Royale*, in 1953, having written it at his Jamaican estate, Goldeneye, where he spent every winter and wrote the Bond novels. While we have mixed feelings about the expression "shaken, not stirred," we are huge fans of the Vesper, the vodka-gin martini that Bond created and named for the double agent Vesper Lynd. In Bond's words he called it after her "because once you have tasted it, you won't drink anything else."

Mountain Cocktail

1½ shots bourbon whiskey • ½ shot dry vermouth
½ shot sweet vermouth • ½ shot lemon juice • ½ fresh egg white

Shake ingredients with ice and strain into chilled glass. Garnish with maraschino cherry.

EVEREST IS FIRST SUMMITED

On this day in 1953, Edmund Hillary and the Nepalese Sherpa Tenzing Norgay became the first climbers to reach the summit of Mount Everest. Tenzing Norgay stated in his narration *The Dream Comes True* that Hillary had indeed taken the first step on top of Everest, despite Hillary's assertions that they both summited at the same time. They were there for just fifteen minutes. In the years that followed, Hillary founded the Himalayan Trust and spent much of his time helping the Sherpa people by building schools and hospitals in Nepal. Sherpas are an ethnic group from the high mountainous region of Nepal and they do the hardest and most dangerous work to help so many climbers up Everest. Today we'd like to remember them, Edmund Hillary and Tenzing Norgay, with a Mountain Cocktail.

Army & Navy

2 shots London dry gin • ½ shot lemon juice • ¼ shot almond (orgeat) syrup • ½ shot cold water

Shake ingredients with ice and strain into chilled glass. Garnish with lemon zest twist.

MEMORIAL DAY

Today's national holiday, formerly called Decoration Day, honors the men and women who died while serving in the country's armed forces. There are parades, people visit cemeteries and memorials, a National Memorial Day Concert is performed on the West Lawn of the U.S. Capitol, the flag is flown at half-mast and a moment's silence is held at 3 PM local time. In honor of this special day, we will be taking a trip back in time, and indulging in a classic, the Army & Navy. We've adapted the wonderful David Embury's formula for this surprisingly subtle drink, which was published in his 1948 *The Fine Art of Mixing Drinks*, and added a twist of our own.

Grassy Finnish

1 chopped fresh lemongrass stem • 2 shots lime-flavored vodka
1 shot spiced honey liqueur • ¼ shot sugar syrup

Muddle lemongrass in base of shaker. Add other ingredients, shake with ice and strain into chilled glass. Garnish with lemongrass.

WALT WHITMAN'S BIRTHDAY

At the time of its publication, Whitman's controversial poetry collection *Leaves of Grass*, with its overt sexuality, was considered by many to be obscene. In fact, the collection is an epic celebration of modern American life that reaches out to the common man. Whitman published the first edition privately in 1855, without his name appearing on the title page, but some way into the text he describes himself as "Walt Whitman, an American, one of the roughs, a kosmos,/Disorderly fleshy and sensual…eating drinking and breeding…" Born on this day in 1819, Whitman was a vocal proponent of the temperance movement, so we hope he won't mind us drinking to his fine poetry with a vodka-based Grassy Finnish.

June

Mimosa

½ shot Grand Marnier
1¾ shots orange juice
top with champagne brut

Pour ingredients into chilled glass and gently stir.
Garnish with orange zest twist.

THE RITZ PARIS OPENS

César Ritz and August Escoffier opened the doors of the Paris Ritz, ancestor to the London Ritz, on the Place Vendôme, to a glittering reception on this day in 1898, and since then the various bars have played host to many celebrated bartenders. For a long time it was home to Coco Chanel, as well as Ernest Hemingway, who, along with a bunch of marines, famously "liberated" it from the Luftwaffe, who had used it as their headquarters during World War II. The Mimosa, a classic champagne cocktail, was created here in 1925 and that's what we'll be drinking today.

Negroni

1½ shots London dry gin • 1½ shots Campari • 1½ shots sweet vermouth

Pour ingredients into ice-filled glass and stir. Garnish with orange wedge.

REPUBLIC DAY IN ITALY

Today Italians will be celebrating the Festa della Repubblica. On this day back in 1946, Italy held a referendum to determine its form of government (monarchy or republic) to follow the end of World War II and the fall of Fascism. The country voted out the king (who had supported Mussolini during the war) and became a republic, and male members of the royal House of Savoy were sent into exile. Why not join Italians in their celebrations with a fine and meditative Italian cocktail, the Negroni? It is thought to date back to 1919, when an aristocrat named Count Camillo Negroni wanted an Americano with "a bit more kick."

Moonshine Martini

1½ shots London dry gin • ½ shot maraschino liqueur • 1 shot dry vermouth • ⅛ shot absinthe

Stir ingredients with ice and strain into chilled glass. Garnish with maraschino cherry.

ED WHITE WALKS IN SPACE

On this day in 1965, in the middle of the Cold War, astronaut Ed White became the first American to walk in space, only a few weeks after his Russian counterpart became the first-ever spacewalker. White floated out of his capsule into space, attached by a 25-foot cord, and maneuvered using a type of gas gun, achieving views of the Earth few had imagined. The order to return from his twenty-three minutes of almost-zero gravity in the emptiness of space was, he said, the saddest moment of his life. We suggest you mark his achievement with a Moonshine Martini, an adult take on the Wet Martini, based on a recipe from Harry Craddock's 1930 *The Savoy Cocktail Book*.

Aunt Emily

1½ shots London dry gin • 1½ shots calvados • ¾ shot apricot brandy liqueur
¾ shot orange juice • ⅛ shot pomegranate (grenadine) syrup

Shake ingredients with ice and strain into chilled glass. Garnish with apricot wedge.

A VERY BRAVE LADY

Emily Wilding Davison bravely stepped out onto the racecourse in front of King George V's horse Anmer at Britain's Epsom Derby on this day in 1913 to draw his and the country's attention to the women's suffrage cause. It's thought that her intention was to attach a sash to the bridle of his mount, but sadly she was hit by the horse and sustained injuries that resulted in her death four days later. Tens of thousands of people lined the streets of London for her funeral, and her coffin was accompanied by thousands of suffragettes. Emily was a fierce campaigner who was jailed on nine occasions and force-fed forty-nine times. You could say that Emily is an aunt to all women who now have the vote, so today we're remembering this brave lady with a forgotten classic, an Aunt Emily.

Green Destiny

1-inch cucumber • ½ fresh kiwi fruit • 2 shots bison grass vodka
1½ shots apple juice • ¼ shot sugar syrup

Muddle cucumber and kiwi in base of shaker. Add other ingredients, shake with ice
and strain into glass filled with crushed ice. Garnish with kiwi slice.

WORLD ENVIRONMENT DAY

World Environment Day was established in 1972. Although Earth Day is arguably a bigger celebration in some circles, World Environment Day counts for a lot around the world, acting as a vehicle for the United Nations in inspiring worldwide awareness and action for the environment. It encourages each and every one of us to do something positive for the environment, with the goal that individual actions as part of a collective power will make a notably positive impact on the planet. This event is about our future and the destiny of our planet, so today we'll be drinking a Green Destiny, a cocktail created in a Polish bar.

Widow's Kiss

1½ shots calvados • ¾ shot Bénédictine D.O.M. liqueur • ¾ shot yellow Chartreuse • 2 dashes bitters

Stir ingredients with ice and strain into chilled glass. Garnish with mint.

D-DAY LANDINGS

Allied soldiers jumped into the sea off the coast of Normandy, weighed down with about 75 pounds of gear, and fought their way through the waves, machine-gun fire and barbed wire, onto the French beaches on this day in 1944. It would take almost another year to bring World War II in Europe to an end, but with Allied forces landed in France, the tide was truly turned. Code-named Operation Neptune, the Normandy landings of 156,000 men on a fifty-mile stretch of the Normandy coast, which was divided into five sectors code-named Utah, Omaha, Gold, Juno and Sword Beach, formed the largest seaborne invasion in history. So that we never forget those brave men, we will drink to them today with a Widow's Kiss, based on Normandy's favorite drink, calvados.

Algonquin

½ ring pineapple • 1½ shots straight rye whiskey • ¾ shot dry vermouth • 1 dash Peychaud's Bitters

Muddle pineapple in base of shaker. Add other ingredients, shake with ice and strain into ice-filled glass. Garnish with pineapple wedge and maraschino cherry.

IN MEMORY OF DOROTHY PARKER

Author, wit and journalist for *The New Yorker*, Dorothy Parker passed away on this day in 1967. Mrs. Parker, who said her favorite words were *check* and *enclosed*, is also often credited with the immortal line, "I must get out of these wet clothes and into a dry martini." Today we are toasting this larger-than-life character with an Algonquin. Our take on this classic cocktail derives its name from the Manhattan hotel at which Mrs. Parker's Algonquin Round Table met to drink, bitch and wisecrack every day for ten years, and is a suitable tribute to the lady herself.

Platinum Blonde

1½ shots aged rum • 1½ shots Grand Marnier • ½ shot whipping cream • ½ shot milk

Shake ingredients with ice and strain into chilled glass. Garnish with grated nutmeg.

THE BIRTH OF UNIVERSAL

The oldest film production company in the U.S., Universal Studios, was established today in 1912 as the Universal Film Manufacturing Company by a German-Jewish immigrant from Wisconsin named Carl Laemmle. He was largely motivated by irritation at Thomas Edison, who refused stars credits and charged high fees to show his movies. Universal survives today in a much changed form, having been sold, merged, de-merged and re-merged many times. To all the beautiful actresses that Mr. Laemmle brought to the silver screen, today we're drinking a Platinum Blonde.

Resolute

1¾ shots London dry gin • 1 shot apricot brandy liqueur • ½ shot lemon juice • ½ shot cold water

Shake ingredients with ice and strain into chilled glass. Garnish with lemon zest twist.

MALLORY AND IRVINE DISAPPEAR

In 1923, George Mallory wrote, "The first question which you will ask and which I must try to answer is this, 'What is the use of climbing Mount Everest?' and my answer must at once be, 'It is no use.' There is not the slightest prospect of any gain whatsoever." On this day in 1924, during the third British attempt to summit Everest, George Mallory and Andrew Irvine were lost for good on its northeast ridge, last seen more than 800 feet below the top. Mallory's body was found in 1999, but neither Irvine's body nor the camera he was carrying has been recovered, and climbing historians continue to obsess over their deaths. These two brave men, who climbed into the unknown with homemade oxygen apparatus, really do deserve celebrating with an appropriately named Resolute.

Last Word

1½ shots London dry gin • ½ shot green Chartreuse
½ shot maraschino liqueur • ½ shot lime juice • ¼ shot cold water

Shake ingredients with ice and strain into chilled glass. Garnish with lime wedge.

THE BIRO PATENTED

Working as a journalist in Hungary, Bíró László József noticed that newspaper ink dried quickly and smudge-free. Finding that the same ink was too thick to flow into the tip of a fountain pen, he worked with his brother to develop a rolling ball in a socket that would pick up ink from a cartridge and then roll it onto paper. During the war the brothers moved to Argentina, and today in 1943 they filed a patent and formed Biro Pens of Argentina. Their new pen was licensed for production in the U.K. to supply Royal Air Force aircrew, who found that the pens worked better at altitude than fountain pens. And what do all those Biros do? They write words, so today we're drinking an aptly named Last Word.

Horse's Neck with a Kick

2 shots bourbon whiskey • 3 dashes bitters • top with ginger ale

Pour ingredients into ice-filled glass and stir. Top with ginger ale. Garnish with lemon zest twists.

THE GREEKS MAKE IT INTO TROY

According to calculations by Eratosthenes, a Greek scholar from the third century BC, on this day in 1184 BC Troy was sacked and burned by revenging Greeks. They had sailed to Troy to bring back Helen, stolen by Paris of Troy from Menelaus, the king of Sparta, ten years previously. The Greeks, still unable to infiltrate the city, had built a huge, hollow wooden horse, left it outside the city gates and pretended to sail away. The unwitting Trojans dragged the horse into the city, and after darkness Greek soldiers, hidden inside, crept out and opened the gates. Thus the Trojans had brought about their own destruction. It may all be fiction, of course, but in thanks for a great story, today we're drinking a Horse's Neck with a Kick.

Caipirinha (Contemporary Serve)

¾ fresh lime • 2 shots cachaça • ½ shot sugar syrup

Muddle lime in base of shaker. Add cachaça and sugar syrup. Shake with 6 oz. crushed ice and pour into glass without straining. Garnish with lime wedges.

INTERNATIONAL CACHAÇA DAY

As today is both Dia dos Namorados (Brazil's answer to Valentine's Day) and International Cachaça Day, it's the perfect occasion to acquaint yourself with the Brazilian national drink, which also happens to be cachaça. This particular day was earmarked to celebrate cachaça because it was on this date, in 1744, that Portugal, then the colonial power in Brazil, outlawed both the making and selling of cachaça. If you're not *au fait* with cachaça's flavor potential, we recommend you try it in a Caipirinha, pronounced "kie-pur-reen-yah." The name of this traditional Brazilian cocktail translates as "little countryside drink."

Tailor Made

1 teaspoon runny honey
1½ shots bourbon whiskey
¼ shot falernum liqueur
1 shot pink grapefruit juice
1 shot cranberry juice

Stir honey with bourbon in base of shaker to dissolve honey. Add other ingredients, shake with ice and strain into chilled glass. Garnish with grapefruit zest twist.

SEWING MACHINE DAY

They're kind of mundane so we don't think about them much, but the sewing machine is one of man's greatest inventions and without one you probably wouldn't be wearing what you've got on today. Sewing is making a comeback and the sewing machine, once a standard item in most households, is, too. They can be tricky to thread, so if you're having trouble with yours, why not take a break, mix yourself a Tailor Made and go back to the task later?

Sandygaff

⅔ glass Guinness
splash of ginger ale

Pour ale into glass, top with ginger ale and lightly stir.

SANDPAPER WAS PATENTED

Sandpaper is a simple enough invention but invention it is, and it was patented in 1834 by one Isaac Fischer Jr., of Springfield, Vermont. Anyone who has ever had to prep a piece of wood for painting will know how important a piece of sandpaper is. So pat yourself on the back for all the do-it-yourself you've ever done, but give it a miss today and instead enjoy an appropriately named Sandygaff.

Royal Smile

1 shot London dry gin
1 shot calvados
½ shot lemon juice
¼ shot pomegranate (grenadine) syrup
½ shot cold water

Shake ingredients with ice and strain into chilled glass. Garnish with lemon zest twist.

SMILE POWER DAY

It's not just humans who smile—most mammals do, too, and scientists have suggested that the smile is a way of expressing harmlessness to predators. Smiles are international—they are understood by everyone, regardless of culture, race or religion. The smile is so important and can change so much in a moment that we think it should be celebrated today on Smile Power Day with a Royal Smile.

Thriller Martini

2 shots blended scotch whisky • ¾ shot London dry gin • ¾ shot orange juice • ¼ shot sugar syrup

Shake ingredients with ice and strain into chilled glass. Garnish with orange zest twist.

BIRTHDAY OF THE ROLLER COASTER

Back in 1884 a new form of entertainment took off on this day at New York's Coney Island: the roller coaster. Inspired by a mining railway in Pennsylvania, and similar to the mine cart railway in the film *Indiana Jones and the Temple of Doom*, only slower, the new coaster, known as the Switchback Railway, was powered by gravity and reached speeds of six mph. Marcus Thompson's patented invention proved popular, and other entrepreneurs piled in with their own improvements. Still running today, the 1902-built Leap the Dips, in Lakemont Park, Pennsylvania, is similar to the original Switchback Railway. This evening we're suggesting you skip the roller coaster and get all the fun you need from a Thriller Martini, a remarkably aromatic combo of scotch, gin and a hint of orange.

New York, New York

1½ shots bourbon whiskey • ¾ shot apple schnapps liqueur
¾ shot sweet vermouth • 1 dash whiskey barrel-aged bitters

Stir ingredients with ice and strain into chilled glass. Garnish with maraschino cherry.

STATUE OF LIBERTY DELIVERED

The Statue of Liberty, a gift to the American people from France, arrived in New York City's harbor today in 1884 aboard a French ship. For her transatlantic journey, the 151-foot-tall statue had been disassembled and divided among more than 200 packing cases. She was rebuilt and on October 28, 1886, one of the world's most recognizable icons took her place on Bedloe's Island. When Ellis Island, next door, became the prime reception point for immigrants to the United States, the Statue of Liberty was the first sight that greeted the optimistic voyagers to the land of the free and she became the international symbol of New York. Today we're toasting the great lady with—what else?—a New York, New York.

Dry Ice Martini

2 shots vodka • ½ shot dry vermouth
¾ shot ice wine

Stir ingredients with ice and strain into
chilled glass. Garnish with orange zest twist.

ICELANDIC
INDEPENDENCE DAY

Today is Iceland's National Day, commemorating Iceland's independence from Denmark in 1944. Icelanders will enjoy the day with parades (some of them headed by Iceland's stumpy little ponies) and by consuming a range of somewhat unusual traditional dishes that take in rotten shark, acid-cured seal flippers, sheep's heads and rams' testicles. They will also imbibe quite a lot of the national spirit, a clear, unsweetened schnapps called Brennivin (or Black Death). We, on the other hand, have chosen to drink to Iceland and Icelanders with what we think of as a more civilized drink, a Dry Ice Martini.

Gin Salad
Dry Martini

2½ shots London dry gin
½ shot dry vermouth
1 dash orange bitters

Stir ingredients with ice and strain
into chilled glass. Garnish with green olives
and cocktail onions.

MARTINI DAY

Whether, like James Bond, you like your martini stirred not shaken, or not, as today is National Martini Day you now have the perfect excuse to enjoy one. Our preferred recipe is a synthesis of two executions: the Gibson, with two cocktail onions, and the classic Dry Martini, with gin and olives. On such a special day we'll be combining both, and enjoying a Gin Salad Dry Martini, with olives and onions.

Noble Europe

1½ shots Tokaji Hungarian wine
1 shot vodka • 1 shot orange juice
1 dash vanilla extract

Shake ingredients with ice and strain into
glass filled with crushed ice. Garnish with
orange slice.

THE CHANNEL TUNNEL
OPENS

First thoughts of a channel tunnel, probably motivated by a desire to invade Britain, began in France as far back as 1751. In the mid-19th century, a French engineer dived to below 98 feet to research the geology of the channel. In the 1880s, British and French teams started digging, but the British army, still suspicious of the invasion risk, called a halt to the project. It wasn't until this day in 1993, after seven years' hard work, that the first train crossed between France and England. We're toasting the event with an aptly named Noble Europe.

Night and Day

½ shot Grand Marnier • ½ shot Campari • top with champagne brut

Pour ingredients into chilled glass. Garnish with orange zest twist.

GREENLAND NATIONAL DAY

Also known as Ullortuneq, meaning "the longest day," Greenlanders chose today as their national day precisely because it is the longest and lightest day of the year. As part of the celebrations, the country is decked out with the Greenlandic flag, which comprises a red semicircle, representing the midnight sun, set on a white background for the ice. Islanders dress in their brightly colored traditional beaded costumes and celebrate with singing, folk dances, kayaking and Greenlandic food parties. As night and day are pretty much the same thing in Greenland on this date, we think it's only appropriate to raise a champagne-topped Night and Day.

He's at Home

½ shot lime juice • 2 shots green Chartreuse • 1 dash mint bitters

Shake ingredients with ice and strain into glass filled with crushed ice. Garnish with lime zest twist.

BILBO BAGGINS GOES HOME

At last Bilbo Baggins, unwilling star of J. R. R. Tolkien's *The Hobbit*, makes it back home to Bag End in Shire Reckoning after the long Quest of Erebor, only to learn that he has been declared dead. Poor chap, we think he probably needs a He's at Home cocktail.

Olympic

1¼ shots Cognac V.S.O.P. • 1¼ shots Grand Marnier • 1¼ shots orange juice

Shake ingredients with ice and strain into chilled glass. Garnish with orange zest twist.

FOUNDING OF THE OLYMPIC GAMES

What a great legacy 1894 has left us, because it was on this day in that year that the International Olympic Committee was founded in Paris, on the initiative of Baron Pierre de Coubertin. The baron's ideology was that the competition itself was more important than the winning, as he articulated: "The important thing in life is not the triumph but the struggle, the essential thing is not to have conquered but to have fought well." In thanks for all the tremendous entertainment that the Olympics have given us through the years, today we're drinking an Olympic.

Quebec

2 shots Canadian whiskey • 2 shots Dubonnet Red • 2 dashes orange bitters

Stir ingredients and strain into chilled glass. Garnish with orange zest twist.

FÊTE NATIONALE DU QUÉBEC

The Quebec National Holiday takes place in Montreal and in other areas of French Canada on the same day as the feast day of the Nativity of St. John the Baptist, patron saint of French Canadians. It's a public holiday, and celebrations take in solemn ceremonies as well as live music concerts, sporting events, parades, fireworks and more. Today's delicious cocktail is made with Canadian whiskey, which tends to be lighter in style, and is called none other than a Quebec.

Papa Bear

◆

1 teaspoon honey sugar syrup
1½ shots Cognac V.S.O.P.
1½ shots spiced honey liqueur
¾ shot lemon juice

Shake all ingredients with ice and strain into chilled glass. Garnish with lemon zest twist.

FATHER'S DAY

Father's Day was first observed in West Virginia in 1908 to complement Mother's Day. It is celebrated by many countries on the third Sunday in June. If you can't actually make a drink for your father today, you can certainly make one for yourself to toast his health, and what better drink for Dad than a cognac-based cocktail? This one, named Papa Bear, was created by Tim Homewood at the Dirty Martini Bar in London in memory of an old family friend.

Fish House Punch

1 shot Cognac V.S.O.P. • 1 shot golden rum • ¾ shot crème de pêche
¾ shot lemon juice • ¼ shot sugar syrup • 2 shots cold water

Shake ingredients with ice and strain into ice-filled glass. Garnish with lemon slice and grated nutmeg.

CATFISH DAY

Catfish Day? Whoever knew there was one, and why there even is one…but it does give us the perfect excuse to make our variation on a famous punch recipe, the Fish House Punch, which is believed to have originated at a Philadelphia fishing and social club. Precisely when the drink was first made remains unknown, but cocktail historian David Wondrich says that the first written reference to it appeared in 1794. Whatever its origins, it would originally have been mixed in larger quantities and served from a big bowl. The following poem may be recited when serving this cocktail: There's a little place just out of town/Where, if you go to lunch/They'll make you forget your mother-in-law/With a drink called Fish House Punch.

Violet Affinity

2 shots créme de violette liqueur • 1 shot dry vermouth • 1 shot sweet vermouth

Stir ingredients with ice and strain into chilled glass. Garnish with lemon zest twist.

VIOLETTE SZABO'S BIRTHDAY

A World War II secret agent of immense bravery and beauty, Violette was born in Paris on this day in 1921 and died in Ravensbrück concentration camp in 1945. Born to a French mother and an English father, she went to school in London. She later married a French officer who was killed in the Battle of El Alamein, and it was this sad event that motivated her to become a spy. Parachuted into France, Violette reorganized and led a Resistance network, but on her second mission she was identified by the Germans and arrested. Despite interrogation and torture, she did not betray her comrades. Violette Szabo, we salute you with a Violet Affinity.

Million Dollar Cocktail

2 shots London dry gin • 1 shot sweet vermouth • ½ shot pineapple juice
¼ shot pomegranate (grenadine) syrup • ½ fresh egg white

Shake ingredients with ice and strain into chilled glass. Garnish with orange zest twist.

THE CASHPOINT IS BORN

As with cell phones and computers, it is hard to imagine life without the cash machine, and yet it wasn't so long ago that they weren't around at all. The world's first ATM (automatic teller machine) arrived at Barclays Bank in Enfield, London, on this day in 1967. Japan, Sweden and the U.S. had been working on a similar system, and a deposit machine called the Bankograph had debuted in the U.S., but the Brits were the first with the cashpoint. Today we're saying Happy Birthday to the cash machine with a Million Dollar Cocktail.

Bronx

1½ shots London dry gin • ¾ shot dry vermouth • ¾ shot sweet vermouth • 1 shot orange juice

Shake ingredients with ice and strain into chilled glass. Garnish with maraschino cherry.

INVENTION OF THE SAXOPHONE

It may surprise you to know that the saxophone does have a very precise birthday and that it's today. In 1846, Adolphe Sax patented this new musical instrument. One of music's unsung heroes, Sax learned to make instruments as a child from his father. He personally played both flute and clarinet but felt the need for a new instrument that was softer than brass and more penetrating than woodwind and the sax really is the best of both worlds. The saxophone would go on to become a jazz staple, so tonight we're opting for a famous Jazz Age cocktail: Johnny Solon's Bronx. Created at New York's Waldorf Astoria, Solon allegedly named it for the Bronx Zoo, because some of his customers had told him about the strange animals they saw after a lot of mixed drinks.

Cable Car

2 shots spiced rum • 1 shot triple sec • ½ shot lemon juice • ¼ shot sugar syrup • ½ fresh egg white

Shake ingredients with ice and strain into chilled glass. Garnish the rim with cinnamon and sugar.

SAN FRANCISCO'S BIRTHDAY

People have lived on the site of San Francisco since at least 3000 BC and there were Native American villages in the bay when the first Spanish explorers arrived, but it was on this day in 1776 that Spanish colonists first established the Mission of San Francisco of Assisi. Starting out as a sleepy little place, the city expanded hugely during the Gold Rush of 1848, when gold was found in its streams. What better way to mark San Francisco's anniversary, and its many fabulous bars, than with a Cable Car cocktail? It was created by Tony Abou-Ganim at San Fran's twenty-one-story-high Starlight Room in reference to the bar's catchphrase, "between the stars and the cable cars."

London Cocktail

2½ shots London dry gin • ⅛ shot absinthe • ⅛ shot sugar syrup • 2 dashes orange bitters
½ shot cold water

Shake ingredients with ice and strain into chilled glass. Garnish with orange zest twist.

TOWER BRIDGE OPENS

After eight years of construction, London's Tower Bridge was opened today in 1894 by the Prince of Wales, the future King Edward VII. As a fixed bridge would have cut off access for tall-masted ships, the new bridge over the river Thames was designed with spans that could rise up. The bridge still takes priority over road traffic and over the years there have been several incidents, including a double-decker bus that had to leap the gap in 1952 when the bridge started to lift midcrossing, a couple of aircraft that dared to fly under its spans in 1968 and 1973, and the notorious division of President Bill Clinton's motorcade when he was separated from his police escort in 1997. Tower Bridge sums up everything that's great about London, so today we're drinking to this lovely bridge with a London Cocktail.

July

Bloody Caesar

2 shots vodka • 4 shots Clamato juice
½ shot lemon juice • 7 drops Tabasco
3 dashes Worcestershire sauce
2 pinches celery salt • 2 grinds black pepper

Rock rather than shake ingredients in a shaker
with ice and strain into ice-filled glass. Garnish with
lemon slice and green bean.

NATIONAL BIRTHDAY

It may seem odd that a drink invented in Canada
took the name of Rome's most famous emperor,
but while the Bloody Caesar's origins are Canadian, its
inspiration is decidedly Italian. Charged with inventing
a signature drink to celebrate the opening of a new
Italian restaurant, Walter Chell recalled a Venetian
pasta dish blending tomatoes and clams. Add in the
requisite Worcestershire sauce and other spices, and
the result is a Bloody Mary with a real kick. The typical
finish to a Bloody Caesar is to wet the rim with lemon
juice, then turn the glass upside down and dip in celery
salt; serve with a slice of lime. However, the finish of the
cocktail is where you can be adventurous, as this cocktail
works with almost any garnish. Use your imagination!
The Bloody Caesar has been known to be served with
anything from olives and peppers to pickled vegetables
and even shrimp. So if you think something will work,
it probably will. Here we have gone for the elegant
and deliciously crunchy green bean. But whatever
garnish you choose, Canada's unofficial national drink
is perfect for celebrating the nation's birthday, or for
fending off the Barbarian horde...depending on which
kind of Caesar you are.

Death in the Afternoon

¼ shot absinthe • ½ shot lemon juice • ¼ shot sugar syrup • top with champagne brut

Shake first three ingredients with ice and strain into chilled glass. Top with champagne.
Garnish with rose petal.

IN MEMORY OF ERNEST HEMINGWAY

Nobel Prize–winning author, war correspondent, big-game fisher, bullfighter and all-around macho man, Ernest Hemingway died on this day in 1961. One of the world's most notorious drinkers, Hemingway famously hung out at the Paris Ritz and Harry's Bar in Venice. Today we've chosen to celebrate the great man's life and mark his sad passing with a cocktail of his own invention: Death in the Afternoon. Aptly named after Hemingway's nonfiction book about bullfighting, this potent blend of absinthe and champagne made its debut in a 1935 book of cocktails, *So Red the Nose*, by famous authors. We've toned down the maestro's original recipe a little, as it included a whopping amount of absinthe.

Islander

2 shots sweet vermouth • ¾ shot blended scotch whisky • ¼ dash Pernod

Stir ingredients with ice and strain into chilled glass. Garnish with lemon zest twist.

PITCAIRN AHOY!

Today in 1767 fifteeen-year-old midshipman Robert Pitcairn, on board the British sloop HMS *Swallow*, sighted the islands that were to take his name. Pitcairn Island went on to achieve notoriety in 1790, when nine mutineers from Captain Bligh's HMS *Bounty* and their Tahitian companions settled there and set fire to the stolen ship. They'd long since set Captain Bligh and a few loyal men adrift in a twenty-three-foot launch. About fifty people currently live on the island, some of whom are thought to be descendants of the original settlers. Because we wish we could find ourselves washed up on a lovely island, just for a day or two, today we'll be drinking an Islander.

Americano

2 shots Campari
2 shots sweet vermouth
top with soda

Pour Campari and vermouth into ice-filled glass and top
with soda. Stir. Garnish with orange zest twist.

INDEPENDENCE DAY

The Fourth of July commemorates the Founding
Fathers' Declaration of Independence from
Great Britain on this day in 1776. Back then
the United States of America comprised just
thirteen states—the former colonies—so the
first Independence Day celebrations featured
thirteen-gun salutes. Today a "salute to the union"
comprises a fifty-gun salute, which is fired at noon
on many military bases. July Fourth is a federal
holiday, and the day will be marked with parades,
fireworks, picnics, barbecues, concerts, baseball
games, political speeches and ceremonies. Today
we will be drinking to everything that's great about
America with an Americano, a drink that was first
served at Gaspare Campari's bar in Milan and was
originally known as the Milano-Torino. It was
during Prohibition that the Italians noticed an influx
of Americans who particularly enjoyed the drink
and so dubbed it the Americano.

Bikini Martini

2 shots London dry gin • ¼ shot peach schnapps liqueur • ¾ shot blue curaçao liqueur
¼ shot lemon juice • ½ shot cold water

Shake ingredients with ice and strain into chilled glass. Garnish with orange zest twist.

BIKINI DAY

The bikini made its debut under its current name courtesy of an automobile engineer named Louis Réard in 1946. Réard was responding to a competition to create the world's smallest swimsuit, and the design he created was so daring for the times that he couldn't find a fashion model to wear it. Instead, Micheline Bernardini, a nude dancer, did the honors on this day at a Paris swimming pool, the Piscine Molitor, and the white buttocks exposed by the G-string back of the design would gain her more than 50,000 fan letters. Your goal for today is to get to the closest beach to mark the day with a Bikini Martini, a drink created by Dick Bradsell for an Agent Provocateur swimwear party at the end of the 20th century.

Bull's Blood

½ shot light white rum • 1 shot Cognac V.S.O.P. • 1 shot Grand Marnier • 1½ shots orange juice

Shake ingredients with ice and strain into chilled glass. Garnish with orange zest twist.

PAMPLONA: THE RUNNING OF THE BULLS

The beginning of the festival of San Fermín is marked at noon today in the city of Pamplona, Spain, with a rocket launched from the town square. From tomorrow morning at 8 AM, and at the same time every morning until July 14, the festival's most famous feature, the notoriously dangerous Pamplona bull-run, will take place. Thousands of people will test their courage and wit against two herds of bullocks plus six wild bulls, each weighing at least 1,100 to 1,320 pounds, stampeding through the town's narrow streets. Since records began, fifteeen people have died in Pamplona and more than 200 have been injured. To the competitors in this epic event we'll be wishing them the best of luck with a Bull's Blood, a well-balanced cocktail infinitely more palatable than its name suggests.

Alien Secretion

2 shots vodka • ½ shot melon liqueur • ½ shot coconut rum liqueur • 3 shots pineapple juice

Shake ingredients with ice and strain into ice-filled glass. Garnish with pineapple wedge and maraschino cherry.

THE ROSWELL UFO

An air force surveillance balloon crashed at a ranch near Roswell, New Mexico, today in 1947. The incident went on to become the center of a variety of increasingly elaborate theories alleging that an extraterrestrial spaceship was involved in the accident. The military, wanting to conceal the fact that the balloon was in the air to detect Soviet nuclear testing, reported it as a conventional weather balloon. It was this cover-up that led to speculations in the late 1970s that alien spacecraft with extraterrestrial occupants had crash-landed and that the military had hidden it away. For us, this day simply must be celebrated, because this extraordinary-looking 1980s cocktail, an Alien Secretion, just had to be in this book.

The Business

2 shots London dry gin • ½ shot honey water (2:1) • ½ shot lime juice

Shake ingredients with ice and strain into chilled glass. Garnish with lime zest twist.

THE *WALL STREET JOURNAL* HITS THE STREETS

The origins of the *Wall Street Journal* lie in a series of bulletins that were issued throughout the working day and delivered by hand to traders on the New York Stock Exchange by the Dow Jones & Company. These were then compiled at the end of the day into the Customers' Afternoon Letter and it was this compilation that later became the *Wall Street Journal*, first published today in 1889. It currently has the highest newspaper circulation in the country and has won a Pulitzer Prize thirty-four times, reason enough, we think, to toast it with a gin-based cocktail, The Business, to say Happy Birthday to this long-standing publication.

JULY 9

Roadrunner

2 shots tequila • ¾ shot lemon juice
2 dashes bitters • ½ shot maple syrup
½ fresh egg white

Shake ingredients with ice
and strain into chilled glass. Garnish
with lemon zest twist.

"RUN, FORREST, RUN"

It's the birthday of Tom Hanks, star of a magnificent portfolio of movies including *Forrest Gump, Saving Private Ryan, Cast Away* and the *Toy Story* series. In 2014 Hanks was reported by one newspaper as the highest-grossing actor in film history. His acting career began in school and has continued on an ever-ascending path. He made living history when Asteroid 12818 Tomhanks was named after him. Tonight we'll be watching one of our favorite movies, *Forrest Gump*, with a Roadrunner in one hand and a table-tennis paddle in the other.

JULY 10

Piña Colada

2 shots golden rum
3 shots pineapple juice
⅔ shot cream of coconut
½ shot lime juice

Blend ingredients with 12 oz.
of ice. Garnish with pineapple wedge
and maraschino cherry.

PIÑA COLADA DAY

Piña Colada, which means "strained pineapple," has been the official national drink of Puerto Rico since 1978, and the nation celebrates its creation each year on this day. There are two main styles of Piña Colada: the earlier, Cuban style, which is rum and pineapple with a hit of lime and sugar, and the later, Puerto Rican style, blended with additional cream of coconut. You can add extra dimension to the pineapple by charring it first, and add body to the drink as a whole by using a hefty rum.

JULY 11

Triple C Cocktail

2 shots vanilla-infused vodka
1 shot dark crème de cacao liqueur
1¼ shots cranberry juice

Shake ingredients with ice and strain
into chilled glass. Garnish the rim with
cocoa powder.

DONALD BRADMAN SCORES 309 IN ONE DAY

Donald Bradman scored an extraordinary 309 runs against England today during the 1930s Ashes cricket series. This remains the highest score by a batsman in one day. At the end of his innings he had scored 334, the first of his two triple centuries. For many, Bradman is the greatest batsman of all time—when he retired in 1948, he had an incredible batting average of 99.94, still way beyond what any batsman has achieved since. In memory of Bradman's extraordinary cricketing achievement, today we are drinking a Triple C Cocktail.

Jumpin' Jack Flash

1½ shots Tennessee whiskey • ½ shot crème de banane liqueur
½ shot Galliano L'Autentico liqueur • ¾ shot orange juice • ¾ shot pineapple juice

Shake ingredients with ice and strain into chilled glass. Garnish with pineapple wedge.

THE ROLLING STONES' FIRST GIG

Mick Jagger, Keith Richards, Brian Jones, Ian Stewart and Dick Taylor, billed as the Rollin' Stones, played their first gig on this day in 1962, at the Marquee Club on London's Oxford Street. The genesis of the Rolling Stones dates back to kindergarten, where the young Mick Jagger and Keith Richards were friends. Hooking up again as teenagers, they formed a band. Though death, marriage and egos have changed the lineup over the years, the gist and the sound remain the same. From "Paint It Black" to "Mother's Little Helper," and from "Satisfaction" to "Sympathy for the Devil," the Stones have produced some of the most memorable tracks of classic rock— including "Jumpin' Jack Flash," for which today's cocktail is named.

Hollywood

1½ shots light white rum • ½ shot pink grapefruit juice
⅛ shot pomegranate (grenadine) syrup • ½ fresh egg white

Dry shake ingredients. Shake again with ice and strain into chilled glass. Garnish with grated nutmeg.

THE BIRTHDAY OF HOLLYWOOD

In 1923, a bunch of California real-estate agents established a company to sell property up in the Hollywood Hills. At a cost of $21,000, they set up on Mount Lee an enormous, illuminated sign that read "Hollywoodland." Formally dedicated on this day, the national landmark has had its low points over the years. In the 1930s, a failed actress committed suicide by jumping from the sign. By 1949, it was in disrepair and missing the "H." When the Hollywood Chamber of Commerce restored it, it regained the "H" but lost the "land." In 1976, the sign was amended by cannabis campaigners to read "Hollyweed," and in 1978 it was demolished and replaced with the structure we have today. We are toasting it, and everything to do with Tinseltown, with an excellent cocktail, the Hollywood.

French 75

1½ shots London dry gin
½ shot lemon juice
¼ shot sugar syrup
top with champagne brut

Shake first three ingredients with ice and strain into chilled glass. Top with champagne. Garnish with lemon zest twist.

BASTILLE DAY

Known as both La Fête nationale and Le quatorze juillet, Bastille Day in France today is celebrated with Europe's oldest and largest regular military parade (which in recent years has come to include French allies). The day commemorates the 1789 storming of the Bastille, an event that marked the beginning of the French Revolution. The people of Paris, whose voice in the form of the National Assembly was only just beginning to be heard, had become fearful that they would be attacked by the royal army. Therefore, seeking to gain ammunition and gunpowder and to free political prisoners, they stormed the fortresslike Bastille prison, which had become a symbol of the absolutism of the monarchy, and freed its prisoners. The day also commemorates the Fête de la Fédération, a celebration that was held a year after the storming of the Bastille to mark the unity of the French people. Today we are drinking one of the greatest and most historic of all cocktails: a French 75.

Diamond Dog

1 shot Campari
1 shot dry vermouth
1 shot lime cordial
1 shot orange juice

Shake ingredients with ice and strain into ice-filled glass. Garnish with orange slice.

PET FIRE SAFETY DAY

It has been mentioned by Reuters, so it must be a real day. If you have a beloved pet, it's worth thinking about, as pets do die in house fires, and domestic fires can be caused by inquisitive pets. If you leave a pet at home, make sure you leave him near a door so that he can be rescued and ensure that he can't chew on electrical wires. And, of course, when you practice your fire drill, make sure you remember to include your pet. He is precious, and that's why today we will be drinking a Diamond Dog cocktail.

Opening Act

2 shots ginger liqueur ◆ ½ shot Campari
½ shot lime juice ◆ 1 dash orange bitters
top with tonic water

Shake first four ingredients with ice and strain into ice-filled glass. Top with tonic water. Garnish with mint.

MI5 BECOMES A LESSER-KEPT SECRET

Today, in 1993, a senior British government employee named Stella Rimington posed for a photocall outside MI5 headquarters, thus launching a new era of openness. This is because Rimington was the director general of MI5, the internal British security service, which was previously so secret that its existence couldn't be acknowledged. If you've ever wondered why M suddenly became a woman in the James Bond movies, Rimington is why—Judi Dench's M was based on her. Today we are toasting Rimington and the opening of those doors with an Opening Act.

Gin Punch

2 shots London dry gin
¾ shot freshly squeezed lemon juice
¾ shot sugar syrup
2 shots chilled water
1 dash bitters

Shake ingredients with ice and strain into ice-filled glass. Garnish with lemon slice.

FIRST EDITION OF *PUNCH*

The first edition of *Punch* was published on this day in 1841. Its founders wanted to create content that was of a higher literary standard and less bitter than other British comic publications. The name *Punch* was settled on when someone remarked that the magazine should be like a good Punch mixture—nothing without Lemon (referring to Mark Lemon, the magazine's first editor)—whereupon founder Henry Mayhew shouted, "A capital idea! Let us call the paper *Punch*!" Today we are drinking to the memory of this great magazine with a Gin Punch.

Hunter

2½ shots bourbon whiskey • ½ shot cherry brandy liqueur • ⅛ shot maraschino liqueur
3 drops orange bitters

Stir ingredients with ice and strain into chilled glass. Garnish with maraschino cherry.

HUNTER S. THOMPSON'S BIRTHDAY

The father of gonzo journalism, Hunter S. Thompson, of *Fear and Loathing in Las Vegas* fame, was born today in 1937. Thompson came up with the immortal phrase "I hate to advocate drugs, alcohol, violence or insanity to anyone, but they've always worked for me." At his funeral, his ashes were fired from a cannon at the top of a tower shaped like a fist holding a peyote button, one of his favorite hallucinogens. Thompson generally enjoyed his bourbon neat, but we think he might also have appreciated the bourbon-based cocktail we are drinking today: a Hunter.

Daiquiri No. 1 Natural

2½ shots light white rum • ¾ shot lime juice • ½ shot sugar syrup
½ shot cold water • 2 slices lime peel

Bitter lime zest oils are key to the balance of this drink. Hence, peel lime before squeezing, then add two slices (cut pole to pole) of lime peel with other ingredients. Shake with ice and strain into chilled martini glass. Garnish with lime wedge.

DAIQUIRI DAY

Bars the world over will be celebrating Daiquiri Day today. While the combination of rum, lime and sugar is very old—dating back to the early days of the British navy and probably before—the mining engineer Jennings Cox is usually credited with the invention of the Daiquiri (pronounced "dye-ker-ree"), possibly at the Venus Hotel in Santiago de Cuba. Yet the true master of the Daiquiri was a Catalonian–Cuban named Constantino Ribalaigua Vert of Havana's famous Floridita bar. We're marking today with our own 10:3:2 formula, a Daiquiri No. 1 Natural.

Tres Amigos Daiquiri

1 shot tequila • ¼ shot navy rum • ½ shot lime juice • ¼ shot sugar syrup

Shake ingredients with ice and strain into chilled glass. Garnish with lime wedge.

DÍA DEL AMIGO

Día del Amigo, or Friend's Day, is celebrated in Argentina, Brazil and Uruguay in acknowledgment of the wonderful thing that is friendship. Though not actually a public holiday, the event is pretty huge in these countries—you'll probably need to make a reservation if you want a table in a restaurant, and the mobile network has been known to collapse under the weight of all the well-wishing. If you have a friend you haven't seen for a while, tonight is the night to get things moving and invite him or her over for a Tres Amigos Daiquiri.

Moonwalk

¾ shot Grand Marnier • 2 dashes orange flower water • 3 dashes grapefruit bitters
top with champagne brut

Pour ingredients into chilled glass. Top with champagne. Garnish with orange wedge.

MEN WALK ON THE MOON

Buzz Aldrin and Neil Armstrong, two-thirds of the crew of the Apollo 11 mission, became the first men to walk on the moon on this day in 1969. As Armstrong stepped on to the lunar surface he uttered his famous words, "One small step for [a] man, one giant leap for mankind." They spent about two and a half hours outside the spacecraft and collected forty-seven-and-one-half pounds of lunar material to bring back to Earth. In honor of space explorers past, present and future, we are drinking a Moonwalk, created at the London Savoy in 1969.

Nessie

1½ shots blended scotch whisky • ¼ shot Islay whisky • ¾ shot sweet vermouth
¼ shot walnut liqueur • ⅛ shot Pedro Ximénez sherry • 2 dashes whiskey barrel-aged bitters

Stir ingredients with ice and strain into chilled glass. Garnish with orange zest twist.

LOCH NESS MONSTER ACHIEVES FAME

The sighting of the Loch Ness Monster by Mr. and Mrs. George Spicer on this day in 1933 is our particular favorite as Nessie was actually out of the loch. Although the monster had been spotted before, national interest was particularly sparked when Spicer and his wife saw "a most extraordinary form of animal" cross the road in front of their car and enter Loch Ness. A lot of people have dedicated a lot of time to seeking out the Loch Ness Monster (who lives in a Scottish lake that contains more water than all the lakes in England and Wales put together), and we think they, and the Spicers, should be applauded—if for nothing else than the entertainment they've given us—with a very Scottish-tasting Nessie cocktail.

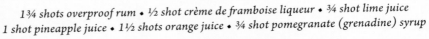

Reggae Rum Punch

1¾ shots overproof rum • ½ shot crème de framboise liqueur • ¾ shot lime juice
1 shot pineapple juice • 1½ shots orange juice • ¾ shot pomegranate (grenadine) syrup

Shake ingredients with ice and strain into ice-filled glass. Garnish with pineapple wedge and maraschino cherry.

HAILE SELASSIE'S BIRTHDAY

Haile Selassie, African statesman, global icon and the last emperor of Ethiopia, was born today in 1892. Before he became emperor, his title was Ras Tafari, a name which forms the heart of Rastafarianism. Some believers in the Rastafari movement worship Haile Selassie as a messiah—either God incarnate or the reincarnation of Jesus—though others believe that he was simply an earthly king chosen by God. The Rastafari movement began in Jamaica during the 1930s. Many of its followers use cannabis spiritually and reject Western society, calling it Babylon, along the lines of the movement's most famous adherent, Bob Marley. Though many Rastas do not drink alcohol, today we are enjoying a very Jamaican drink, the Reggae Rum Punch.

Amatitan Twist

2 shots tequila • ¼ shot maraschino liqueur • ¼ shot yellow Chartreuse • 2 dashes grapefruit bitters

Stir ingredients with ice and strain into chilled glass. Garnish with grapefruit zest twist.

NATIONAL TEQUILA DAY

Bars across the country will be knocking out Margaritas in honor of the Mexican national spirit, and as fans of the blue agave juice, we are certainly joining in because today is National Tequila Day in the U.S. Our drink of the day will be an Amatitan Twist. Why an Amatitan? Well, Amatitán, in Jalisco, is home not only to one of Mexico's largest distilleries but also to what's possibly its oldest one—the early-18th-century Taberna El Tecuane, in Santa Rosa canyon, where you can see huge fermentation pots carved into the rock. These early distilleries were set up in remote spots because the Spanish authorities, wishing to protect the sales of Spanish brandy, had outlawed liquor production in Mexico.

Suffering Bastard

1 shot light white rum • 2 shots rhum agricole • ½ shot orange curaçao liqueur
¼ shot almond (orgeat) syrup • ½ shot sugar syrup • 1 shot lime juice

Shake ingredients with ice and strain into glass filled with crushed ice. Garnish with pineapple cubes, maraschino cherry, lime wedge and mint.

ADMIRAL NELSON LOSES AN ARM

Not only did Rear Admiral Horatio Nelson lose the Battle of Santa Cruz de Tenerife on this day in 1797, but he lost his arm as well. The British were attempting a beach landing followed by a ground attack on the Spanish port but they were mown down by Spanish cannon, mortar and guns, many of which were manned by civilians. Nelson is reported to have said, pointing to his right arm, "Doctor, I want to get rid of this useless piece of flesh here." Following amputation, the arm was thrown overboard, despite the admiral's wish to keep it. We're sure Nelson would have needed a stiff drink—we'd have offered a Suffering Bastard.

Evita

2 shots vodka • ½ shot melon liqueur • 1 shot orange juice • ½ shot lime juice

Shake ingredients with ice and strain into chilled glass. Garnish with orange zest twist.

DEATH OF EVA PERÓN

María Eva Duarte de Perón died on this day in 1952, at just thirty-three. Born poor and illegitimate, Eva rose from B-movie actress to first lady of Argentina as the second wife of President Juan Perón. Known locally as Evita, she became a cult figure and helped women gain the right to vote in Argentina. When she died, her body was mummified, buried, later exhumed, and moved several times, also spending time in Peron's dining room. It is now back in Buenos Aires in a very secure tomb, so nervous are the authorities that it will be stolen by adoring fans. Today we're drinking to this legendary woman with an Evita.

Breakfast Martini

1 teaspoon marmalade • 2 shots London dry gin • ½ shot triple sec • ½ shot lemon juice

Stir marmalade with gin in base of shaker until it dissolves. Add other ingredients, shake with ice and strain into chilled glass. Garnish with orange zest twist and toast triangle.

SLEEPYHEAD DAY

Oh, those crazy Finns! In Finland today is Sleepyhead Day, when the last person in the house in bed is woken with a bucket of cold water or an involuntary dip in a lake or river. In the town of Naantali, one local celebrity will begin the day by being carried, still in nightclothes, to the sea and then dunked. We can think of many more pleasant ways to start the day than a drenching in cold water, and just one of them is with a Breakfast Martini, world-renowned Salvatore Calabrese's eminently palatable blend of marmalade, gin and orange.

Pisco Punch

3 cloves • 2 shots pisco • 1 shot pineapple juice • ½ shot orange juice
½ shot lemon juice • ½ shot sugar syrup • ½ shot champagne brut

Muddle cloves in base of shaker. Add next five ingredients, shake with ice and strain into ice-filled glass. Top with champagne. Garnish with pineapple wedge.

PERUVIAN INDEPENDENCE DAY

The next couple of days are huge in Peru as the nation gets two days off from work to commemorate the country's liberation from the Spanish empire. On this day in 1821 General José de San Martín proclaimed Peru's independence. This extraordinary man, Argentinian by birth, had studied in Spain, taken part in the Peninsular Wars and then returned to South America for a whirlwind liberation campaign that crossed South America and included the liberation of Chile. Any day is a good day to drink a Pisco Punch, a cocktail based on the brandy named for a Peruvian town, but today is the perfect day. The early origins of this cocktail are shrouded in mystery, but it makes a firm appearance in San Francisco in 1853 at the Bank Exchange bar. Our Pisco Punch adds cloves.

Starry Night

2 shots dry white wine • ½ shot poire William eau de vie • ½ shot maraschino liqueur

Stir ingredients with ice and strain into chilled glass. Garnish with star anise.

VAN GOGH DIES

Tragically, Vincent van Gogh shot himself today in 1890. Although his paintings now sell for tens of millions, van Gogh sold only one during his entire lifetime, trading many for food, art supplies and accommodation. Whether he actually cut off his own ear or whether it was severed in a fight with fellow artist Paul Gauguin, no one knows—though he did present it melodramatically to a local prostitute before almost dying of blood loss. Some attribute van Gogh's eccentricities to his consumption of absinthe, which at that time contained a higher quantity of psychoactive ingredients than is legal today. But today we're going to leave out the absinthe altogether and remember one of Vincent's finest paintings with a Starry Night cocktail.

Classic Cocktail

2 shots Cognac V.S.O.P. • ½ shot Grand Marnier • ½ shot maraschino liqueur
½ shot lemon juice • ½ shot cold water

Shake ingredients with ice and strain into chilled glass. Garnish with lemon zest twist.

PENGUIN BOOKS DEBUT

The paperback revolution began on this day in 1935 with the publication of ten Penguin books. They were the inspiration of Allen Lane, who, traveling home from a weekend visiting Agatha Christie in Devon, was frustrated by the lack of cheap but good fiction available at the Exeter railway station. The original Penguin books were color-coded and included works by Ernest Hemingway, Dorothy L. Sayers and Agatha Christie. Each one cost just six pence, at a time when hardcovers were priced at seven or eight shillings. The new concept was an instant success and Lane went on to launch Penguin as a standalone publisher in 1936. Within a year, Penguin had sold three million paperbacks, many of which would go on to become classics, so today we'll be drinking none other than a Classic Cocktail.

Grog

2 shots navy rum • ½ shot lime juice • ½ shot muscovado sugar syrup
2 shots cold water • 2 dashes bitters

Shake ingredients with ice and strain into ice-filled glass. Garnish with lime wedge.

BLACK TOT DAY

On this day in 1970, the British navy retired one of its longest-standing traditions—the midday rum ration, or tot. By the time of its abolition, the tot had been reduced to a mere two-and-one-half fluid ounces of rum, but even that came to be considered too much for men who might spend the afternoon managing weapons and complicated machinery. In the earliest days of the rum ration, however, men were issued with a stunning half pint, which is ten fluid ounces—at a time when its strength would have been north of 57% ABV. We will be marking Black Tot Day with our take on the classic navy drink: Grog. The lime in the original Grog was most likely dished out to prevent scurvy—contributing to British sailors' nickname, Limeys.

August

Chocolarita

2 shots tequila
¼ shot dark crème de cacao liqueur
¼ shot coffee liqueur
1 shot lime juice • ¼ shot sugar syrup

Shake ingredients with ice and strain into chilled glass. Garnish the rim with cocoa powder.

HAPPY BIRTHDAY, SWITZERLAND!

In early August 1291, representatives of Switzerland's different cantons met in a field above Lake Lucerne and joined forces to work against the Austrian occupiers of their country. Today, communities across Switzerland remember this, the starting point of Swiss independence, as they celebrate their national day with bonfires and barbecues. Fireworks illuminate the Alps, light shows flicker on Rhine waterfalls, and small children walk with lanterns through mountain villages. Switzerland will always mean chocolate to us, so we are celebrating with a Chocolarita—a Margarita enriched with both coffee and chocolate.

Wild Irish Rose

2 shots Irish whiskey
½ shot lemon juice
¼ shot sugar syrup
¼ shot pomegranate (grenadine) syrup
½ shot soda

Shake first four ingredients with ice and strain into chilled glass. Top with soda. Garnish with lemon zest twist and maraschino cherry.

HELLRAISER MAKES HIS DEBUT

One of the original hellraisers, alongside his pals Richard Harris and Richard Burton, Peter O'Toole was born in Connemara, Ireland, on this day in 1932. Iconic movies like *Lawrence of Arabia* and *The Last Emperor* made him famous, though his partying exploits were just as legendary. O'Toole once went out for a drink in Paris and woke up in Corsica. He advised a young Michael Caine never to ask what he had done the night before, as "it's better not to know." We are toasting this wild Irishman with a Wild Irish Rose, based on his homeland's native whiskey.

Submarine Kiss

⅓ shot crème de violette liqueur
2 shots London dry gin
½ shot lemon juice
¼ shot sugar syrup
½ shot egg white

Pour liqueur into base of chilled glass. Dry shake rest of ingredients. Shake again with ice and strain slowly into liqueur-primed glass so contents of shaker float over liqueur.

NAUTILUS UNDER THE NORTH POLE

Navigating under the North Pole is no mean feat, but at 11:15 PM on August 3, 1958, Captain Anderson and the crew of the USS *Nautilus* submarine did exactly that—despite magnetism confusing conventional guidance systems and there being absolutely nothing to see. They discovered that the Arctic Sea stretched more than two-and-one-half miles below the North Pole's ice floes. Anderson hoped that passenger submarines would one day ply the route. They don't—yet his achievement deserves celebrating with the aptly named Submarine Kiss.

Strawberry on Acid

3 fresh strawberries
1½ shots vodka
¾ shot crème de fraise liqueur
⅛ shot balsamic vinegar
1 pinch black pepper
top with champagne brut

Muddle strawberries in base of shaker. Add next four ingredients, shake with ice and strain into chilled glass. Top with champagne. Garnish with balsamic-covered strawberry.

DOM PÉRIGNON DRINKS THE STARS

Come quickly, I am drinking the stars!" the Benedictine monk Dom Pérignon allegedly exclaimed when, on the suspiciously precise date of August 4, 1693, he supposedly invented sparkling champagne at his abbey in Hautvillers, France. It's true that the dom was an outstanding winemaker who pioneered a number of champagne innovations, from corks and thicker glass to the successful use of red grapes. Yet sparkling wine would not become the dominant style until long after his death, and some historians suggest it was actually invented and certainly first bottled by the British. That said, Dom Pérignon is a man who merits celebration, so we are toasting him with a Strawberry on Acid, a strawberry fizz concoction made infinitely more interesting by adding balsamic vinegar and black pepper.

Test Pilot

1½ shots aged rum • ¾ shot light white rum • ¼ shot triple sec
¼ shot falernum liqueur • ¼ shot lemon juice

Shake ingredients with ice and strain into ice-filled glass. Garnish with lime zest twist.

NUCLEAR ARMS RACE SLOWS

At the height of the Cold War, on this day in 1963 the United States, the USSR and Britain made a historic move toward world peace by agreeing to the first-ever nuclear test ban treaty. The Moscow treaty banned all testing in the air, in the water or, for that matter, in outer space, although it did allow for underground tests. Within a few months, more than a hundred other nations signed up to the treaty, an important step in halting the nuclear arms race. Let's raise a toast to our safer world, and the international public pressure that led to the treaty, with a Test Pilot, a nuclear-strength Daiquiri packed with cheeky Tiki flavors.

Savoy Special

2 shots London dry gin • 1 shot dry vermouth
¼ shot pomegranate (grenadine) syrup • ⅛ shot absinthe • ½ shot cold water

Shake ingredients with ice and strain into chilled glass. Garnish with orange zest twist.

THE SAVOY'S BIRTHDAY

With all due ceremony, theatrical impresario Richard D'Oyly Carte opened the doors of a brand-new hotel in the heart of London's theaterland today in 1889: The Savoy. He would go on to hire, in a stroke of genius, César Ritz, who brought with him the celebrated chef Auguste Escoffier. For many, the heart of the Savoy is its American Bar. From Ada Coleman to Harry Craddock and beyond, the American Bar has produced some of the world's great bartenders, one of the world's classic cocktail books and myriad fantastic drinks. Our cocktail pick for today is the splendidly classic Savoy Special, an elegant, dry-martini-style affair that appears in Harry Craddock's rightly celebrated 1930 cocktail compendium, *The Savoy Cocktail Book*.

Ramos Gin Fizz

2 shots London dry gin • ½ shot lemon juice • ½ shot lime juice • ¾ shot sugar syrup • ⅛ shot orange flower water • 3 drops vanilla extract • 1 fresh egg white • 1 shot whipping cream • soda from siphon

Flash blend first eight ingredients without ice. Pour contents of blender into shaker and shake with ice. Strain into chilled glass (no ice) and top with soda from siphon. Garnish with lemon slice and mint.

BIG EASY BARTENDER BORN

The man who is arguably New Orleans's most famous bartender, Henry Charles Ramos, generally known as Carl, made his appearance on this day in 1856 in Indiana, to parents of German descent. A Freemason, teetotaler and pillar of society, Ramos wasn't your typical saloonkeeper, especially not in the louche surroundings of Gilded Age New Orleans. Yet he brought the world one of the very few cocktails to have made a specific saloon and bartender famous—the painstakingly shaken Ramos Gin Fizz. During his heyday, Ramos employed entire chains of bar staff passing shakers from hand to hand, to ensure that his famous fizz was fully emulsified. So why not gird your loins, roll up your sleeves and break out your finest hard shake in honor of Carl and his lusciously fragrant mix?

Million Dollar Margarita

1½ shots tequila • 1½ shots Grand Marnier • ½ shot lime juice

Shake ingredients with ice and strain into ice-filled glass. Garnish with lime wedge.

DOLLAR DEBUTS

During the 1700s, the first worldwide currency appeared. And, no, it wasn't the U.S. dollar but a Spanish silver coin with a value of eight Spanish reales, known to anyone who has ever watched a pirate movie as "pieces of eight" and to its users simply as the dollar. Then, confusingly, on this day in 1787, the fledgling United States of America introduced its very own currency, the U.S. dollar, an invention about as American as apple pie. Mix up a Million Dollar Margarita in its honor. With "rested" (reposado) tequila and rich Grand Marnier, it's really quite luxurious.

Singanpore Sling

1½ shots London dry gin
⅓ shot cherry brandy liqueur
⅛ shot Bénédictine D.O.M. liqueur
⅛ shot triple sec
½ shot pineapple juice
1 shot lemon juice
⅛ shot sugar syrup
1 dash bitters
1 dash orange bitters
top with soda

Shake first nine ingredients with ice and strain into
ice-filled glass. Top with soda and stir. Garnish with lemon
slice and maraschino cherry.

SINGAPORE NATIONAL DAY

Very few countries are blessed with an instantly recognizable national cocktail—yet Singapore, which celebrates its independence from Malaysia today, is permanently associated with the Singapore Sling, a staple in bars across the city-state. The spiritual home of the Singapore Sling is, of course, the Raffles Hotel, a vast, colonial Christmas cake of a hotel whose Long Bar has played home to stars and literati from Joseph Conrad and Rudyard Kipling to Noël Coward, Charlie Chaplin and Ava Gardner. Sadly, the Singapore Slings served in the Long Bar today are a very far cry from the original drink that Hainan-Chinese bartender Ngiam Tong Boon created, perhaps back in 1915. This take on the long-lost original recipe incorporates the Singapore Sling's key ingredients—Cherry Heering liqueur, fresh pineapple, citrus, Bénédictine, gin, grenadine, bitters, triple sec and soda—in a refreshing, nonsyrupy long drink.

Singapore Sling

RAFFLES
HOTEL

Navigator

2 shots London dry gin • ¾ shot limoncello liqueur • 1¼ shots pink grapefruit juice

Shake ingredients with ice and strain into chilled glass. Garnish with lemon zest twist.

MAGELLAN HEADS AROUND THE WORLD

One of the world's greatest navigators and captains, the Portuguese explorer Ferdinand Magellan set out from Seville, Spain, on this day in 1519, in command of five Spanish ships. His mission was to circumnavigate the globe. Only one of Magellan's ships, *The Victoria*, would survive the three-year ordeal, along with just eighteen of its original crew. Although the expedition completed its mission, Magellan did not make the entire voyage, as he was killed during the Battle of Mactan in the Philippines in a premature attempt to convert the natives to Christianity. In honor of a great explorer and the epic voyage that bears his name, we are drinking a Navigator: a citrusy, accessible Martini.

Mayan Whore

2 shots tequila • ¾ shot coffee liqueur • 1½ shots pineapple juice • top with soda

Shake first three ingredients with ice and strain into ice-filled glass. Top with soda, DO NOT stir. Garnish with pineapple wedge.

MAYAN LONG COUNT STARTS

The world was meant to end on December 21, 2012—at least according to the Mayan Long Count calendar, which began today in 3114 BC. Our favorite contribution from that mysterious Central American civilization, however, is not the calendar, but agave, the plant we have to thank for tequila. Mayans believed that a god named Two Rabbits gave up his life so that humans could drink fermented agave. That was rather kind of Two Rabbits, and today is the perfect day to toast him with a Mayan Whore, a seductive tequila blend enriched with both coffee and pineapple.

Pussyfoot

7 fresh mint leaves • 4 shots orange juice • ½ shot lemon juice • ½ shot lime juice
½ shot pomegranate (grenadine) syrup • 1 fresh egg yolk

Muddle mint in base of shaker. Add other ingredients, shake with ice and strain into ice-filled glass.
Garnish with orange slice.

CAT-PONDERING PHYSICIST BORN

Erwin Schrödinger, the Austrian physicist who brought us the brain-exploding experiment known as Schrödinger's Cat, was born on this day in 1887. In his (fortunately) hypothetical experiment, a cat is placed in a sealed box with a Geiger counter, radioactive material and poison; if the counter detects radioactive decay, the cat is poisoned. The question is whether, without an observer there to influence its state, the cat is dead or alive. And, yes, if you're a quantum physicist, that's a very important question, indeed. We are easing our now rather tired brains with a suitably feline nonalcoholic cooler, the Pussyfoot.

Boilermaker

1 shot bourbon whiskey • 1 pint Pilsner lager

Pour whiskey to brim of shot glass and then maneuver shot glass so it is held tight up against the inside base of an upturned Boston glass. Then quickly flip the Boston glass over so that the bourbon is trapped in the now upside-down shot glass. Now pour beer into Boston glass over the whiskey-filled shot glass.

STAINLESS STEEL INVENTED

Since the very first smith melted metal and shaped it into something new, pioneers have raced to discover new materials. On this day in 1913 an English metallurgist named Harry Brearley achieved a goal that others had long strived for: a new steel alloy, so resistant to everything from nitric acid to lemon juice and vinegar that Brearley, rather unimaginatively, christened it "rustless steel." The substance we now know as stainless steel is used in everything from chemistry to bartending. We're celebrating it with a favorite drink of Pennsylvania steelworkers, the bourbon and beer combo known as a Boilermaker.

Jack Collins

2 shots calvados • 1 shot lemon juice • ½ shot sugar syrup • top with soda

Shake first three ingredients with ice and strain into ice-filled glass. Top with soda, stir.
Garnish with lemon slice.

CARLOS THE JACKAL CAPTURED

For years, the Marxist–Leninist terrorist Ilich Ramírez Sánchez was one of the most wanted men in the world, and by the time he was captured in Sudan on this day in 1994, he had assassinated secret agents, masterminded a bombing campaign and taken sixty to seventy innocents hostage at an oil conference. The media dubbed him "the Jackal" after Frederick Forsyth's classic thriller *The Day of the Jackal*. Today he is serving two life sentences, a fact for which we should all be grateful, as it provides the perfect excuse for a classic long drink, the Jack Collins.

Flower Power Martini

2 shots London dry gin • ½ shot elderflower liqueur • ½ shot dry vermouth
¼ shot créme de violette liqueur

Shake ingredients with ice and strain into chilled glass. Garnish with orange zest twist.

WOODSTOCK SETS THE TONE

Billed as "an Aquarian exposition: 3 days of peace & music," and still probably the world's most famous music festival, Woodstock kicked off today in 1969, and more than half a million hippies turned up. Artists including Janis Joplin, The Who, Jimi Hendrix and The Grateful Dead took to the stage at a farm in upstate New York, while festivalgoers stripped naked to swim in the swamp, roll in the mud or avail themselves of the services of the dedicated "bad trip tent." As flower power goes, Woodstock has never been surpassed and will probably never be forgotten, so we're remembering it with the floral but potent Flower Power Martini.

Rum Punch

2¼ shots overproof rum
¾ shot lime juice
1½ shots sugar syrup
3 dashes bitters
3 shots cold water

Shake ingredients with ice and strain into glass filled with crushed ice. Garnish with orange slice and maraschino cherry.

NATIONAL RUM DAY

Today is National Rum Day. Yet, for the dedicated rumhound, wherever they may be, every day is a rummy day, as W. C. Fields might have said. Once the favored hooch of pirates, slave-traders and—so far as the categories could be distinguished—the British navy, rum has come a long, long way since it was first known as kill-devil. We're celebrating Rum Day with the ultimate rum cocktail, the rightfully long-lived Rum Punch. This recipe follows the Jamaican style, using strong overproof rum over crushed ice to dilute its intensity but the classic punch proportions: one of sour, two of sweet, three of strong and four of weak. If serving from jugs or, even better, a classic punch bowl, use ice cubes to prevent overdilution.

Mae West

2 shots vodka
½ shot amaretto liqueur
¼ shot melon liqueur
1½ shots cranberry juice

Stir ingredients with ice and strain
into chilled glass. Garnish with melon slice.

MAE WEST BORN

When choosing between two evils, I always like to pick the one I never tried before," Mae West once remarked. The ultimate brassy blonde, Mae West was born on this day in 1893 in Brooklyn, New York. Known for her bawdy double entendres, she first made a name for herself as a vaudeville star and then moved to Hollywood, where she repeatedly came up against the censors. Her view was "I believe in censorship. I made a fortune out of it." The Mae West Martini, a delicious hot pink cherry–chocolate confection, is the perfect tribute to the queen of the high life.

Up in the Air

2 shots vodka • ½ shot apple juice
½ shot lemon juice
¼ shot almond (orgeat) syrup

Shake ingredients with ice and strain
into chilled glass. Garnish with apple and
lemon slice.

HELIUM FOUND IN THE SUN

The French astronomer Pierre Janssen traveled all the way to India to observe the total eclipse of the sun that occurred on this day in 1868. As the moon crept across the face of the sun, he detected an unusual color band in the sunlight and concluded that it must indicate an unknown element. Later that year a British astronomer named Norman Lockyer would observe that selfsame color and propose the element be called helium, after Helios, the Greek name for the sun. It was 1895 before someone finally isolated helium on earth. Why not mark the fantastic element that makes balloons stay up in the air with a fruity Up in the Air?

Aviation Cocktail

1¾ shots London dry gin
½ shot maraschino liqueur
¼ shot crème de violette liqueur
½ shot lemon juice
¼ shot cold water

Shake ingredients with ice and strain into
chilled glass. Garnish with lemon zest twist
and sugar rim (optional).

NATIONAL AVIATION DAY

In 1939 President Roosevelt declared that airplane pioneer Orville Wright's birthday would be National Aviation Day. And since that's today, we're celebrating Orville's 1871 birth with one of the most accessible vintage cocktails, the Aviation, a product of that heady era when flights were very far from routine. The Aviation recipe appeared not long after Wright's first-ever powered flight, when Hugo R. Ensslin, head bartender at New York's Wallick Hotel, included it in his 1916 cocktail book, *Recipes for Mixed Drinks*.

Paradise

1 fresh passion fruit • 2 shots London dry gin • ¾ shot apricot brandy liqueur ¾ shot orange juice

Halve passion fruit, scoop out seeds and flesh into shaker. Add other ingredients, shake with ice and strain into chilled glass. Garnish with orange zest twist.

PARADISE LOST PUBLISHED

Today in 1667 the poet John Milton's publisher, Samuel Simmons, registered a poem entitled *Paradise Lost* with the British Stationer's Office, and one of the greatest works of English literature became official. Milton, however, received a total of just £20 for his blank-verse epic on the temptation of Adam and Eve and the fall of man from grace. A philosopher as well as a poet, a passionate Republican and a believer in religious freedom, Milton was truly a man ahead of his time. We are remembering his legacy by getting lost in a Paradise.

Mona Lisa

1 shot green Chartreuse 3 shots orange juice • 2 dashes bitters top with tonic water

Shake first three ingredients with ice and strain into ice-filled glass. Top with tonic water. Garnish with orange wedge.

THEFT MAKES MONA LISA'S NAME

For all her famous smile, and for all Da Vinci's talents, it is intriguing that the *Mona Lisa* has become the world's most famous artwork. It was on this day in 1911 that her status became assured, when Vincenzo Peruggia crept out of a broom closet in Paris's Louvre museum, unhooked the painting and carried it out under his clothes. The ensuing furor made the artwork globally famous, and by the time a Florence art dealer reported Peruggia, the *Mona Lisa* was an icon. A splendid excuse, we think, to enjoy a long and fruity Mona Lisa.

French Mule

2 shots Cognac V.S.O.P. • 1 shot lime juice • 1 shot sugar syrup • 3 dashes bitters • top with ginger beer

Shake first four ingredients with ice and strain into ice-filled glass. Top with ginger beer, stir. Garnish with mint.

ENTER HENRI CARTIER-BRESSON

The father of photojournalism, Henri Cartier-Bresson was born today in 1908, in Chanteloup-en-Brie, France. His belief that "in photography, the smallest thing can be a great subject. The little human detail can become a leitmotiv" would shape photography for decades, helping found the now-commonplace reportage style. Bilingual, brave and an all-around intellectual, Cartier-Bresson packed away his camera in the mid-1970s to devote himself to painting. The French Mule, a spicy, flavor-packed take on the classic Moscow Mule, is the perfect tribute to this French icon.

Blood and Sand

1 shot blended scotch whisky • ¾ shot cherry brandy liqueur • ¾ shot sweet vermouth
1 shot orange juice • ⅛ shot Islay whisky

Shake ingredients with ice and strain into chilled glass. Garnish with orange zest twist.

HEARTTHROB DIES TRAGICALLY

The first great heartthrob of an era, the beautiful Rudolph Valentino, died of appendicitis today in 1926 at the age of only thirty-one. Valentino's magnetism was such that an estimated 100,000 people lined the streets of New York City to pay their respects at his funeral, and some fans reportedly committed suicide. He was a talented actor, dancer and boxer, led an actors' strike against the studios, published a book of poetry and recorded two songs. Today's drink, one of the iconic scotch cocktails, takes its name from the film *Blood and Sand*, one of the top four grossing movies of 1922, in which Valentino plays a bullfighter torn between his childhood sweetheart and an aristocrat's seductive daughter. Naturally, he expires tragically at the end.

Old Flame

1 shot London dry gin • ½ shot triple sec • ½ shot sweet vermouth • ¼ shot Campari
1½ shots orange juice

Shake ingredients with ice and strain into chilled glass. Garnish with orange zest twist.

VESUVIUS ERUPTS

The eruption of Vesuvius in AD 79 was bad news for the folks of Pompeii and Herculaneum, but great news for the archaeologists who discovered the towns either drowned in ash or flooded by mud but otherwise untouched, complete with rude graffiti, brothels and all. Today was also not a good day for the writer Pliny, whose uncle died while evacuating citizens from the shadow of the volcano, causing Pliny to record the day in epic detail. A tragedy for the victims, today's eruption was a bounty for future generations. It's also an excellent excuse for Dale DeGroff's mouthwatering—and flame-colored—Old Flame, a very adult riff on the classic Bronx.

Whiskey Sour

2 shots bourbon whiskey
1 shot lemon juice
½ shot sugar syrup
3 dashes bitters
½ fresh egg white

Shake ingredients with ice and strain into ice-filled glass.
Garnish with lemon slice and maraschino cherry.

WHISKEY SOUR DAY

Today is Whiskey Sour Day. A classic cocktail that was already an old drink when Jerry Thomas first recorded a recipe in his 1862 cocktail book *Bar-tender's Guide*, the Whiskey Sour has never been truly fashionable and so has never become unfashionable, either. One of those rare drinks that works all year round, it has enough bourbon body for autumn and winter, yet is refreshing enough for spring and even high summer. Raw egg white might seem like a random addition, yet it's actually essential. As the egg white emulsifies while you shake, its proteins slowly unfurl, creating a silky mouthful that both smooths and lengthens the drink.

Parma Violet Spritz

3 shots sparkling wine • 2 shots créme de violette liqueur • top with soda

Pour sparkling wine and liqueur into glass. Add ice. Top with soda. Serve with Parma Violet candies.

NEW COLOR TRANSFORMS SCIENCE

In 1856, a teenage chemistry prodigy, William Perkin, accidentally invented a new color. His discovery, mauveine, which he patented on this day, would go on to change the world, in this case quite literally. Before Perkin's discovery, all dyes were natural—made from roots, leaves, flowers or, in the case of purple, sea snails. Now, for the first time, fabrics could be dyed in predictable, lasting shades. Best of all, Perkin's discovery inspired other bright young Londoners to take up chemistry and develop medicines, photography and much, much more. We are toasting Perkin and his purple with the mauve-colored, violet-flavored Parma Violet Spritz.

Venus in Furs

1 shot raspberry-flavored vodka
1 shot citrus vodka
3½ shots apple juice
3 dashes bitters

Shake ingredients with ice, strain into ice-filled glass. Garnish with berries and lemon slice.

FIRST INTERPLANETARY MISSION

Venus may be named for the goddess of love, but she's a savage planet. The surface temperature reaches over 900°F, the atmosphere is as dense as a deep ocean and the planet is permanently covered in cloud. If humans could breathe the sulfur-laden air, it would stink of rotten eggs. We would know little of this without the Mariner 2 spacecraft, which took off from Cape Canaveral today in 1962, and came within 21,700 miles of Venus on Earth's first interplanetary mission. Long, fruity and refreshing, the eminently quaffable Venus in Furs is the perfect mix to beat even Venus's heat.

Weissen Sour

2 shots bourbon whiskey • 1 teaspoon marmalade • ¾ shot lemon juice
2 dashes orange bitters
top with weisse (wheat) beer

Stir marmalade with bourbon in base of shaker to dissolve marmalade. Add lemon juice and bitters, shake with ice and strain into ice-filled glass. Top with beer. Garnish with lemon slice.

ST. AUGUSTINE'S DAY

Today is sacred to the patron saint of beer, St. Augustine of Hippo. Famous for his prayer "God grant me chastity and self-control, but not yet," Augustine spent his early life having a good time, had a long-term unmarried relationship and became a father out of wedlock. Then, in his thirties, he heard what he believed was God's voice commanding him to read the Bible with the words "take up and read," and he abandoned the high life. We're hoping he'll carry on looking after beer for us today, so we're toasting him in a long, refreshing Weissen Sour beer cocktail.

Corpse Reviver No. 2

¾ shot London dry gin
¾ shot triple sec
¾ shot Lillet Blanc
¾ shot lemon juice
⅛ shot absinthe

Shake ingredients with ice and strain into chilled glass.
Garnish with lemon zest twist.

HARRY CRADDOCK'S BIRTHDAY

Harry Craddock, the Savoy's most renowned bartender and the name behind the famous 1930 publication *The Savoy Cocktail Book*, was born on this day in 1875 in Stroud, England. Harry crossed the Atlantic, worked at iconic New York bars including the Hoffman House and the Knickerbocker Hotel, then returned home, post-Prohibition, complete with a highly marketable American accent, reputation and passport. Despite stints at the Savoy, the Dorchester and Brown's Hotel, Craddock would sadly die in poverty. *The Savoy Cocktail Book* says of the Corpse Reviver No. 2, "Four of these taken in swift succession will unrevive the corpse again." Enjoy one, or possibly two, of this fabulous gin–lemon–absinthe mix in memory of the great man tonight.

The Colonial Cooler

1½ shots London dry gin • 1½ shots sweet vermouth • ⅛ shot Grand Marnier
⅛ shot Amer Picon • 1 dash bitters • top with soda

Stir first five ingredients with ice and strain into ice-filled glass. Top with soda.
Garnish with pineapple wedge and mint.

BIRTHDAY OF BITTERS

Angostura Aromatic Bitters provides the finishing touch to many a cocktail, thanks to its bittersweet herbal tang. Yet it started life, in the city that was then Angostura and is now Venezuela's Ciudad Bolívar, as a medicinal cure for stomach trouble, the creation of Dr. J. B. Siegert in 1824. On today's date in 1921, the company, by then based in Trinidad, constituted itself as Angostura Bitters (Dr. J. G. B. Siegert & Sons) Limited. Made from the original secret recipe today, Angostura Aromatic Bitters is the unsung hero in many drinks, among them our cocktail of the day, The Colonial Cooler. The gentleman adventurer Charles H. Baker Jr. discovered this long cooling drink in the Sandakan Club, Borneo—precisely the type of tropical environment for which Dr. Siegert invented his bitters.

The Stone Place

2½ shots aged rum • ¾ shot lemon juice • ¾ shot orange juice • ¼ shot pomegranate (grenadine) syrup

Shake ingredients with ice and strain into chilled glass. Garnish with grated nutmeg.

SCULPTOR SAYS FAREWELL

The English sculptor and artist Henry Moore, who died today in 1986, is best known for his monumental semiabstract sculptures, most of which are depictions of the human figure. Many of his works are pierced or contain hollow spaces, and his undulating forms are also thought to draw on the landscape and hills of his Yorkshire birthplace. Although Moore achieved both wealth and fame, he tended to live a simple life, choosing to donate most of his income to the Henry Moore Foundation, which continues to support education and the promotion of the arts. Moore worked primarily in wood, bronze and stone, so today we are remembering this inspiring artist with the citrus-based cocktail The Stone Place.

September

Salty Bird

1½ shots light white rum • ¾ shot Campari
1½ shots pineapple juice
½ shot lime juice • ¼ shot sugar syrup
1 pinch salt

Shake ingredients with ice and strain into
ice-filled glass. Garnish with orange slice
and dried pineapple.

CHICKEN BOY
APPRECIATION DAY

This unofficial day celebrates a
well-known landmark on Route
66 that has been described as "the
Statue of Liberty of Los Angeles."
Chicken Boy is a fiberglass statue of a
chicken-headed boy grasping a bucket
of chicken. He stands twenty-two
feet tall and is named after the 1960s
restaurant he first graced. When the
restaurant closed, he went into storage
until a Los Angeles art director found a
suitable location. In 2010, California's
then-governor Arnold Schwarzenegger
recognized him with a Governor's
Historic Preservation Award. Today,
let's salute him with a bittersweet, fruity
sipper, the Salty Bird.

Fireman's Sour

2 shots light white rum
1 shot lime juice
½ shot pomegranate (grenadine) syrup
½ fresh egg white

Shake ingredients with ice and strain into
ice-filled glass. Garnish with orange slice
and maraschino cherry.

LONDON'S BURNING

Late at night on September 2, 1666,
the Great Fire of London broke
out at a bakery in Pudding Lane. It raged
for three days, destroying 80 percent
of London, including 13,200 houses,
87 churches and St. Paul's Cathedral.
On the plus side, it did help put an end
to the bubonic plague, while only six
people are known to have died. There
was no fire department in those days—
although citizens did their best with
fire breaks—so today's anniversary is a
great opportunity to toast firemen
everywhere with a splendid Rum Sour,
the Fireman's Sour.

Red Lion

1¼ shots London dry gin
1¼ shots Grand Marnier
1 shot orange juice • 1 shot lemon juice
⅛ shot pomegranate (grenadine) syrup

Shake ingredients with ice and strain into
chilled glass. Garnish with orange wedge.

LIONHEART CROWNED

Crowned king of England in
Westminster Abbey today in 1189,
Richard I spent no more than about six
months in the country he ruled for a
decade. His main ambition was to go
on crusade, which meant leaving his
kingdom in the hands of others and,
needless to say, losing his power. When
he finally returned in 1194, he had to be
crowned again, in Winchester. His most
famous legacies are probably his defeat
of the brilliant Arab leader Saladin at the
Battle of Arsuf, and his statue outside
London's Houses of Parliament, the
sword of which was bent during World
War II. Richard was known as Richard
the Lionheart because of his military
prowess, so let's toast the Lionheart
with a classic Red Lion.

Webster Martini

2 shots London dry gin
½ shot apricot brandy liqueur
1 shot dry vermouth
½ shot lime juice

Shake ingredients with ice and strain into chilled glass. Garnish with lime zest twist.

WEB STAR INCORPORATED

As Google continues to grow and dominate so many aspects of the world we live in, it could be argued that today's anniversary may yet turn out to be one of the most influential dates in our lifetime. It was today in 1998 that Sergey Brin and Larry Page took their college research project to the next business level and incorporated Google—largely so they could bank a check written by an investor in their company name. In the hopes that if it does come to it, Google will prove to be a benign and kindly dictator rather than the Big Brother some fear, we are drinking a Webster Martini. With its balance of fruit and vermouth, the Webster tastes extremely contemporary, yet *The Savoy Cocktail Book* remarks that it was a favorite on the early 20th-century ocean liner RMS *Mauretania*.

Blushin' Russian

1 shot vodka • ½ shot amaretto liqueur • 1 shot coffee liqueur • 1 shot whipping cream

Shake ingredients with ice and strain into chilled glass. Garnish with coffee beans.

FACIAL HAIR TAXED TO THE MAX

Governments are good at taxing their citizens, but the Russian tsar Peter the Great has to take the prize. On this day in 1698 he introduced a beard tax. Ostensibly he was trying to force a more modern way of living on his population at a time when most western European men went clean-shaven, but in practice, as with most taxes, the main point was revenue. Anyone who chose to avoid the barbers and preserve his beard had to prove he'd paid the tax by carrying a token inscribed with two phrases: "money taken" and "the beard is a superfluous burden." In memory of all those red-faced Russians, may we recommend a Blushin' Russian, a White Russian improved with extra almond?

Mayflower Martini

1½ shots London dry gin • ½ shot elderflower liqueur • ½ shot apricot brandy liqueur
½ shot apple juice • ½ shot lemon juice

Shake ingredients with ice and strain into chilled glass. Garnish with lemon zest twist.

FROM PLYMOUTH TO... PLYMOUTH

The *Mayflower* first set sail for America on around August 5, 1620, but her partner ship, the *Speedwell*, sprang a leak. A couple of weeks later both the *Speedwell* and the *Mayflower* set out again, only for the *Speedwell* to prove unseaworthy yet again. Finally, on September 6 the *Mayflower* embarked from Plymouth, England, on an epic voyage that would terminate in Plymouth, Massachusetts—without the *Speedwell*. Some of the *Speedwell*'s passengers had squeezed on board the *Mayflower*, while others had given up and gone home. In honor of those first few Pilgrims, who fled a religiously intolerant Europe for a new land and freedom, we are drinking the Mayflower Martini, a floral, juicy blend of orchard fruit and flowers.

Caipirinha (Brazilian Style)

¾ fresh lime (fresh whole)
2 shots cachaça
½ shot sugar syrup

Muddle lime in the base of a robust glass.
Pour cachaça and sugar into glass, add ice and stir.
Garnish with lime zest twists.

BRAZILIAN INDEPENDENCE DAY

Almost everyone in Brazil will be celebrating the anniversary of their country's declaration of independence today. Flags, military parades and all-around jubilation mark the Sete de Setembro (Seventh of September), the day in 1822 on which Brazil broke free from Portugal, the colonizing power. Wherever you are, there's no better way to celebrate a Brazilian holiday than with the undisputed national drink, the Caipirinha, based on the national spirit, cachaça. Serve it up Brazilian style—stirred with ice cubes rather than churned with crushed ice—and the flavors will amaze you. We recommend using sugar syrup in place of the more common sugar cube, unless you actually enjoy the grainy texture of partly dissolved sugar.

Ink Martini

2 shots vodka • ½ shot blue curaçao liqueur • 1½ shots cranberry juice

Shake ingredients with ice and strain into chilled glass. Garnish with orange zest twist.

INTERNATIONAL LITERACY DAY

Today UNESCO calls to mind the subject of literacy, which is still a problem for almost a billion adults around the world. And that's not only those for whom, as in China and Japan, literacy involves distinguishing thousands of characters, but even for those who use our simple Western alphabet. In praise of the written word, which brings us everything from cocktail recipes to world news and great literature, we are drinking an Ink Martini. With both blue curaçao and cranberry juice, it's hardly classical and surprisingly far from inky black, yet its subtle flavor may well surprise you.

Appily Married

2 teaspoons runny honey • 2½ shots vodka • ½ shot apple juice

Stir honey with vodka in base of shaker until honey dissolves. Add apple juice, shake with ice and strain into chilled glass. Garnish with cinnamon and sugar rim.

NINE IS THE CHARM

If you're Chinese, today is a remarkably lucky day. In Chinese, 9/9 is pronounced "jiu-jiu," which sounds like "long long" or "for a very long time," so the number 9, thanks to its pronunciation, is associated with longevity and eternality. All of which makes today an especially auspicious date for couples to get married—back on September 9, 2009, tens of thousands of Chinese couples rushed to tie the knot. It all sounds like a great excuse to mix an Appily Married, a honey-apple-vodka blend that works perfectly with the grainy notes of a good wheat vodka.

Arnold Palmer (Mocktail)

3 shots cold English Breakfast tea • 2 shots lemon juice • 1 shot sugar syrup

Shake ingredients with ice and strain into ice-filled glass. Garnish with lemon slice.

GOLF LEGEND ON COURSE

Golf legend Arnold Palmer was born in Latrobe, Pennsylvania, on this day in 1929—he would go on to become one of the most successful sportsmen of all time, winning more than ninety championships, including seven majors and four Masters. Most famously for cocktail geeks, he donated his name to one of the world's best mocktails—an addictive combo of homemade lemonade and iced tea. No slouch at marketing, Palmer markets his own version under the brand name Arnold Palmer Tee. For a true, refreshing flavor, mix your own at home with freshly brewed breakfast tea.

Highlander

2 shots blended scotch whisky • 1 shot sweet vermouth • 1 dash orange bitters

Stir ingredients with ice and strain into chilled glass. Garnish with orange zest twist.

"FREEDOM…"

In Mel Gibson's epic medieval drama *Braveheart*, there's an iconic scene where English knights in chain mail charge Mel's apparently defenseless Scottish warriors, only to be bloodily impaled on a forest of spikes. The Battle of Stirling Bridge, on this day in 1297, didn't happen exactly like that, but it was a game changer—not just for the Scots leader William Wallace, but for knights around Europe. Until that day, a charge by heavily armored knights had been considered as invincible as tanks were during World War I; after that, the rich were as vulnerable as the poor peasants who followed in their wake. We are toasting Wallace, and Scotland in general, with a Highlander, a suitably Scottish blend of scotch, vermouth and bitters.

French Cocktail

2 shots Cognac V.S.O.P. • *1½ shots pineapple juice* • *½ shot black raspberry liqueur*

Shake ingredients with ice and strain into chilled glass. Garnish with pineapple wedge.

ANCIENT ART UNVEILED

Today in 1940, Marcel Ravidat, an eighteen-year-old mechanic from the village of Montignac in France, stumbled on one of the great wonders of the world: the Lascaux Caves, an ancient human habitation lined with wonderfully lifelike paintings of charging stags, galloping horses and leaping bulls. Nobody knows whether the paintings were sympathetic magic or an early form of entertainment—what is certain is that they had survived for around 17,000 years. In honor of those ancient French artists, and the man who discovered them, we are drinking a French Cocktail, an adult but accessible take on the 1990s French Martini.

Chocolate Stinger

2 shots chocolate spirit • *¾ shot white crème de menthe*

Stir ingredients with ice and strain into glass filled with crushed ice. Garnish with mint.

ROALD DAHL BORN

The stories of Norwegian–British author Roald Dahl—such as *Charlie and the Chocolate Factory, James and the Giant Peach, Matilda, The Witches* and more—have delighted generations of children. Yet there was more than sweet stories to the man who entered the world in Llandaff, Cardiff, on this day in 1916. His adult fiction was sinister and dark, he piloted fighters during World War II and he nursed his first wife, the actress Patricia Neal, through a long recovery from brain injury. In honor of a man with both sweet and sharp sides, we recommend a Chocolate Stinger, a mint–choc take on the vintage Stinger.

Gibson Dry Martini

2½ shots London dry gin • ½ shot dry vermouth

Stir ingredients with ice and strain into chilled glass. Garnish with two cocktail onions.

CHEESECAKE KING APPEARS

You don't have to be a fan of pickled onions to enjoy a Gibson Dry Martini, a classic Dry Martini garnished with two cocktail onions in place of the classic olive or twist. And the man who most likely gave his name to this classic martini variation, Charles Dana Gibson, made his debut on this day in 1867. Charles's wildly popular illustrations of busty, feisty Gibson Girls showed generations of American women how to embrace their femininity—and probably inspired Charles Connolly of the Players Club to name a two-onion martini in their honor. Do try one.

Martini with a Spot

2½ shots London dry gin • ½ shot dry vermouth • 1 dash absinthe

Stir gin and vermouth with ice and strain into chilled glass. Carefully pour "spot" of absinthe into center of the drink. Garnish with lemon zest twist.

INTERNATIONAL DOT DAY

Today is about making your mark as part of a global celebration of creativity, courage and collaboration. The concept originated when on this day in 2009 teacher Terry Shay introduced his classroom to Peter H. Reynolds's book *The Dot*. In it, a patient teacher starts a girl on a journey of self-discovery simply by encouraging her to have the confidence in her own ability to put a small dot on a piece of paper. We're taking a grown-up stance on the day and drinking a Martini with a Spot—it includes a spot of absinthe.

Bandera

2 shots tequila • 2 shots lime juice

For Sangrita:
½ shot tomato juice • ½ shot pomegranate juice
¼ shot orange juice • ½ shot lime juice
⅛ shot pomegranate (grenadine) syrup
2 drops Tabasco • 2 dashes Worcestershire sauce
1 pinch salt • 1 grind black pepper

Pour tequila and lime juice into separate shot glasses. To make Sangrita for third glass, shake rest of ingredients with ice and strain into glass. Instruct drinker to sip from all three glasses alternately.

MEXICAN INDEPENDENCE DAY

In town and city squares throughout Mexico last night, officials will have shouted out the "Grito de Delores" ("Cry of Delores") and the names of the heroes of the Mexican War of Independence, while jubilant crowds responded to each line with the cry "Viva Mexico." After fireworks and late-night partying, today will be filled with joyous parades, mariachi music, traditional costumes, sombreros, marches, singing, flags and even more spectacular fireworks. The ceremony honors Father Miguel Hidalgo y Costilla, who made a declaration of rebellion today in 1810 in the small village of Delores, calling on his compatriots to kick the Spanish out of Mexico. Join the celebrations with a Bandera, a three-shot, tricolored combo that merges the hues of the Mexican flag with the nation's favorite flavors: tequila, lime and, of course, the spicy, scarlet sangrita shot.

Damn It Jimmy

1½ shots sake • 1½ shots light white rum
¼ shot fino sherry
¼ shot dry vermouth • ¼ shot sugar syrup

Stir ingredients with ice and strain into
chilled glass. Garnish with stuffed olive.

MORRISON MISBEHAVES

Ed Sullivan wasn't afraid to
showcase young talent on his TV
show, but he probably regretted doing
so today in 1967, when he hosted Jim
Morrison and The Doors. During
rehearsals the band had been told to
change the lyrics of "Light My Fire"
from "Girl, we couldn't get much
higher" to "Girl, we couldn't get much
better," because it was thought that
the line might refer to drugs. Jim, of
course, didn't change the words, and
afterward the band was told that their
six upcoming appearances on the show
were canceled and they were banned for
good. Damn it, Jimmy, how could you?
And that's why today we're drinking a
Damn It Jimmy cocktail!

Greta Garbo

2 shots light white rum
¼ shot maraschino liqueur
½ shot sugar syrup • 1 shot lime juice
⅛ shot Pernod

Shake ingredients with ice and strain into
chilled glass. Garnish with star anise.

I WANT TO BE ALONE

Stunningly beautiful Greta Garbo
was born in Sweden today in 1905.
After the death of her father, she had
to leave school at the age of fourteen,
to take a job in a department store.
Her beauty shone through and she
was soon modeling for the company
and then won a scholarship to attend
drama school. From there, Hollywood
was inevitable and she became one of
the silent era's biggest stars. Later, her
famously gravelly voice made her an
instant success in the talkies. Garbo
never married, though she came close
when she left John Gilbert standing
at the altar in 1927. Tonight we'll be
drinking a Greta Garbo cocktail, named
for this cinema icon.

Twisted Sobriety

1 shot Cognac V.S.O.P.
1 shot poire William eau de vie
top with champagne brut

Stir first two ingredients with ice and strain
into chilled glass. Top with champagne.
Garnish with pear slice.

CHUBBY CHECKER DOES
THE TWIST

Chubby Checker's 1960s cover of
Hank Ballard's song "The Twist"
made No. 1 on the charts on this day in
1960. Not only that but in September
2008 the song topped *Billboard*'s list
of the most popular singles to have
appeared in its Hot 100 since the
list's debut in 1958. Chubby Checker
introduced the world to a dance craze
that still gets everyone on the dance
floor today—before the Twist, grown-
ups did not dance to teenage music.
What a great excuse to mix a Twisted
Sobriety cocktail and get on down to
the dance floor.

Passionate Rum Punch

1½ fresh passion fruits
1½ shots overproof rum
¾ shot lime juice
½ shot sugar syrup
½ shot passion fruit syrup
top with champagne brut

Cut passion fruits in half and scoop out flesh into shaker. Add next four ingredients, shake with ice and strain into glass filled with crushed ice. Stir, then top with champagne. Garnish with passion fruit.

RUM PUNCH DAY

Whether you're a collector of antique punch bowls or just a casual dabbler, the original spirits-based mixed drink, punch, is certainly worth celebrating. The classic punch is, of course, rum punch. There's just something about rum, particularly overproof, that pairs beautifully with the four other ingredients of punch: the sweet, the sour, the spice and the weak. And, whether the word *punch* originates from "panch," the Hindi word for "five," or "puncheon," a container for liquor, we like ours made to the classic proportions: "one of sour, two of sweet, three of strong and four of weak." A very happy Rum Punch Day to you!

Cobbled Raspberry Martini

2 shots vodka • 1 shot Shiraz red wine
⅓ shot sugar syrup • 12 fresh raspberries

Muddle raspberries in base of shaker. Add other ingredients, shake with ice and strain into chilled glass. Garnish with fresh raspberries.

BILBO GOES ON THE ROAD

Nobody, least of all the middle-aged English professor and philologist who wrote it, would have predicted that *The Hobbit* (or its three-part sequel, *Lord of the Rings*) would have the impact it did—particularly at the time when it came out, which is today in 1927. In popular surveys, J. R. R. Tolkien repeatedly ranks among the all-time greats of English literature. Tolkien's hobbits enjoy the finer things in life: beer for everyday occasions, red wine for special guests and fresh berries from the farmland. Let's toast their anniversary with a vintage combination of berries and red wine, the Cobbled Raspberry Martini.

Black Magic

12 fresh red grapes • ½ shot Grand Marnier • top with champagne brut

Muddle grapes in base of shaker. Add liqueur, shake with ice and strain into chilled glass. Top with champagne. Garnish with black grapes.

LAST SALEM HANGINGS

When nine-year-old Betty Parris and her cousin Abigail Williams began having screaming fits, throwing things about the room, making strange noises and contorting themselves, the villagers of Salem, Massachusetts, instantly thought of witchcraft. In a town notorious for both its bickering and its religious intensity—dancing, Christmas and dolls were all forbidden—panic set in. The mass hysteria resulted in the execution of twenty people, most of them women—the last eight of them on this day in 1692. Tonight we are drinking a Black Magic cocktail and thanking our lucky stars for the century we live in.

Cool Martini

1½ shots melon liqueur • 1 shot tequila
1½ shots cranberry juice

Shake ingredients with ice and strain into chilled glass. Garnish with apple slices.

FEMINIST ICON BORN

The first female presidential candidate entered the world on this day in 1838. At age thirty-four, Victoria Martin would run for president as a representative of the Equal Rights Party. And this wasn't Victoria's only first. She was also the first woman to start a weekly newspaper and the first to run a Wall Street brokers' firm—and she did all this after leaving school at eleven, one of ten children of an illiterate mother. The legacy of this passionate advocate of women's rights lives on. We are toasting the very cool Victoria Martin with a Cool Martini.

Fitzgerald

2 shots London dry gin
½ shot sugar syrup
1 shot lemon juice
2 dashes bitters

Shake ingredients with ice and strain into ice-filled glass. Garnish with lemon slice.

HAPPY BIRTHDAY, GATSBY GUY

Published when he was just twenty-four, *This Side of Paradise* catapulted F. Scott Fitzgerald into fame, wealth and an extravagant lifestyle that earned him a reputation as a playboy and tainted his standing as a serious writer. His next novel, *The Beautiful and the Damned*, was a pitch-perfect critique of what became known as the Jazz Age. But it was his final complete work, *The Great Gatsby*, that would ultimately be recognized as the definitive portrait of the Roaring Twenties. Fitzgerald was born on this day in 1896, so today we're remembering him with a stylishly sour Fitzgerald.

Lone Ranger

1½ shots tequila
¾ shot lemon juice
½ shot sugar syrup
top with champagne brut

Shake first three ingredients with ice and strain into ice-filled glass. Top with champagne. Garnish with lemon zest twist.

ONE-HIT WONDER DAY

Today's National One-Hit Wonder Day was established in 1990 by music journalist Steven Rosen. Okay, so we're only talking fifteen minutes of fame, but there have been some great one-hit wonders over the years—think "Always Something There to Remind Me" by the Naked Eyes, Don McLean's "American Pie" or Norman Greenbaum's "Spirit in the Sky." There's something about those songs that catches the zeitgeist of a moment and brings waves of nostalgia for an era when we hear them again, so why not mix a Lone Ranger, pull out the one-hit wonders you've got tucked away in your collection and celebrate One-Hit Wonder Day in style?

Washington Apple

2 shots vodka • ½ shot sour apple liqueur
3 shots apple juice • ¼ shot lime juice
¼ shot pomegranate (grenadine) syrup

Shake first four ingredients with ice and strain into ice-filled glass. Garnish with apple slice.

CONCORDE BREAKS A RECORD

On this day in 1973, the Concorde slashed the transatlantic air-crossing record, making the journey between Washington and Paris in just over three and a half hours and averaging an impressive 954 mph. The supersonic jet was developed and produced under an Anglo-French treaty, with planes supplied to both British Airways and Air France, and its name reflected the agreement between the two nations. Sadly, some three decades after that record-breaking flight, the Concorde was grounded for good. Today we are raising a glass to that magnificent plane and its Washington flight with a long, refreshing Washington Apple.

Vacation Cocktail

2 shots vanilla-flavored vodka
½ shot coconut rum liqueur
½ shot lime juice
1 shot pineapple juice
¼ fresh egg white
¼ shot blue curaçao liqueur

Shake first five ingredients with ice and strain back into shaker. Then dry shake and strain into chilled glass. Then pour blue curaçao into center of drink. It should sink. Garnish with pineapple wedge.

WORLD TOURISM DAY

We don't know where you went on your last vacation, but we're betting it already feels like a long time ago, even if you only got back yesterday. So thank you to the United Nations for creating today's World Tourism Day—not, of course, that any of us like to think of ourselves as tourists, but we do like a dose of sunshine once in a while. So in memory of all those great vacations gone by, and those yet to come, why not join us in a suitably tropical Vacation Cocktail?

The Star

1½ shots calvados
1½ shots sweet vermouth
1 dash bitters

Stir ingredients with ice and strain into chilled glass. Garnish with olive.

SPACESHIPS GO PRIVATE

Risking everything he had gained from the sale of PayPal in pursuit of his ultimate goal—enabling humankind to live on planets beyond Earth—Elon Musk founded the company SpaceX in 2002. And, on this day in 2008, SpaceX's Falcon 1 became the first privately owned rocket to enter Earth's orbit. Since then, the company has continued to break records and is focused on another game-changing breakthrough: developing reusable rockets. Tonight we're gazing upward, thinking about Elon and his team's incredible vision, and enjoying Harry Craddock's 1930s cocktail The Star.

Illusion

2 shots vodka
¾ shot triple sec
¾ shot melon liqueur
2½ shots pineapple juice

Shake ingredients with ice and strain into ice-filled glass. Garnish with watermelon wedge.

ZSA ZSA GOES DOWN

If Zsa Zsa Gabor hadn't existed, you'd have had to invent her. Creator of such peerless lines as "I never hated a man enough to give him his diamonds back" and "I am a marvelous housekeeper—every time I leave a man, I keep his house," the Hungarian–American icon was jailed today in 1989. A police officer had objected to her driving her Rolls without a license but with an open flask of Jack Daniel's, Zsa Zsa slapped him, and history was made. Because they really don't make them like that anymore, we are toasting her magic with an Illusion.

Eden

2 shots vodka
½ shot elderflower liqueur
1½ shots apple juice
top with tonic water

Shake first three ingredients with ice and strain
into ice-filled glass. Top with tonic water. Garnish with
orange zest twist.

FAREWELL, JAMES DEAN

An icon of the 1950s whose roles were the very embodiment of teenage disillusionment, James Dean died on this day at the age of just twenty-four. He was only four years into a career that was already meteoric and provided for his immortality with roles in just three movies: *Rebel Without a Cause*, *Giant* and *East of Eden*. Passionate about cars, Dean took up motor racing in 1954, in a Porsche Speedster, and repeatedly finished in the top three. Tragically, while he was driving his new Porsche Spyder to a race event on the last day of September 1955, an oncoming car veered into his lane and the two vehicles collided head-on. Dean was pronounced dead on arrival at the hospital. So tonight raise a glass to the *East of Eden* star with a long and appropriately cool Eden.

October

New York Flip

1½ shots bourbon whiskey • ½ shot tawny port • 1 fresh egg (white and yolk) • ½ shot sugar syrup

Vigorously shake ingredients with ice and strain into chilled glass. Garnish with grated nutmeg.

NEW YORK PLAZA OPENED

New York's Plaza Hotel opened on this day in 1907. Many decades after Ernest Hemingway uncharitably advised F. Scott Fitzgerald to give his liver to Princeton and his heart to the Plaza, the hotel—along with its bar—remains a New York icon. When it opened, the nineteen-story building, a skyscraper at the time, featured no fewer than 1,650 crystal chandeliers, among other Gilded Age glitter and glitz. The Oak Room, a cocktail destination, was open only to men until Prohibition forced its temporary closure. Appearances in movies ranging from Hitchcock's *North by Northwest* to *The Great Gatsby*, *Funny Girl* and *Arthur* have contributed to the Plaza's fame. Happy Birthday to the Plaza—we are toasting you with a New York Flip.

Sophisticated Savage

2 shots Tuaca • 1 shot cachaça • ½ shot lime juice • ½ fresh egg white

Shake ingredients with ice and strain into ice-filled glass. Garnish with a lime wedge.

THE OPENING OF TWICKENHAM STADIUM

Twickenham Stadium, in southwest London, opened on this day in 1909 with a match between the Harlequins and Richmond rugby union clubs. Constructed on land previously used to grow cabbages, it has been affectionately known as "the Cabbage Patch" ever since. Its agricultural leanings returned to the fore when it was used during World War I to graze cattle, horses and sheep. Owned and operated by the Rugby Football Union (RFU), it is currently the third-largest rugby union stadium in the world and is home ground to the English rugby union team. Its inauguration capacity for 20,000 spectators has grown to 82,000. Today we are raising a toast to all the players who have stepped onto the pitch at Twickenham with (no insult intended) a Sophisticated Savage.

Apple Strudel

1½ shots vanilla-infused vodka • ½ shot blended scotch whisky
½ shot apple schnapps liqueur
½ shot dry vermouth • ½ shot apple juice
¼ shot sugar syrup

Shake ingredients with ice and strain into chilled glass. Garnish the rim with cinnamon and sugar.

GERMAN UNITY DAY

Tag der Deutschen Einheit, or German Unity Day, today commemorates the reunification of Germany and is marked by political speeches, a Bürgerfest (citizens' festival) and plenty of fireworks. After the mass crossings through the Berlin Wall in 1989, East Germany held its first free elections on March 18, 1990. Negotiations then took place between the German Democratic Republic and the Federal Republic of Germany, which culminated in a Unification Treaty, and on this day in 1990 the GDR was incorporated into the FRG. Construction of the wall had begun in August 1961, and although ideological reasons were given, in practice it existed to prevent mass emigration from East to West, and East German police had shoot-to-kill orders to prevent anyone from escaping. In 1989, a series of bungled orders by the authorities and the dissemination of confused information to the public resulted in the massing of thousands of East Germans demanding that guards open the gates. No one in authority was prepared to issue the order to open fire on the crowds, so the vastly outnumbered guards had no way of holding them back. The gates were finally opened, leading to the historic dismantling of the wall. Today we will be celebrating this fabulous day of victory for the people with an Apple Strudel, a cocktail based on Germany's national liquor, apple schnapps, with a taste reminiscent of that most German of pastries, the apple strudel.

Sputnik

1 shot light white rum • 1 shot Cognac V.S.O.P. • 2 shots orange juice • ½ shot sugar syrup

Shake ingredients with ice and strain into ice-filled glass. Garnish with orange slice.

SPACE RACE BEGINS

The space race began in earnest on today's date in 1957, when the Soviet Union launched Sputnik 1, the first human-created device to enter space. An artificial satellite, only about the size of a beach ball, Sputnik was the forerunner of the 3,000 or so satellites that orbit the Earth today—and the opening gambit in the race that would lead to men walking on the moon and the International Space Station. West of the Iron Curtain, the launch caused more consternation than celebration, as many feared that the Soviet Union would use satellites as a platform to launch nuclear missiles. Happily they didn't, so we will be celebrating that, plus humankind's first venture into space, with a Sputnik.

Love Me Flip

1 fresh egg yolk • ¼ shot sugar syrup • 2 shots aged rum • 1 shot yogurt liqueur
½ shot Pedro Ximénez sherry • 3 drops bitters

Beat egg yolk with sugar in base of shaker. Add other ingredients, shake with ice and strain into chilled glass. Garnish with grated nutmeg.

FIRST BEATLES SINGLE

The first single by the Beatles, "Love Me Do," was released in the U.K. on this very day in 1962. It only reached No. 17 on the U.K. charts, but their second single, "Please Please Me," went to No. 1. Lennon and McCartney had worked on the song when they first formed the band at school, and the Beatles had already been gigging for two years, mainly in Liverpool and Hamburg. Within a year, Beatlemania was in full swing. This was the first time Britain had seen teenage girls near hysteria at the prospect of getting close to their idols. Within two years the Beatles had cracked the U.S., and within seven years John Lennon would have left the band for good. We're toasting the Beatles with a creamy Love Me Flip.

Alice in Wonderland

1 shot Grand Marnier
½ shot tequila

Refrigerate ingredients, then layer in chilled glass by carefully pouring in the above order. Garnish with lime wedge.

MAD HATTER DAY

The Mad Hatter in *Alice's Adventures in Wonderland* wears, as we all know, a top hat. On that top hat is a price label that bears the words "in this style 10/6," meaning that the hat, if ordered, would cost 10 shillings and sixpence. Here in the U.S., 10/6 means October 6—and that is why today is Mad Hatter Day, a day for general silliness and definitely a day to drink an Alice in Wonderland cocktail.

Cuba Libre

3 shots cola
2 shots golden rum
¼ shot lime juice
2 dashes bitters

Pour ingredients into ice-filled glass and lightly stir. Garnish with lime wedge.

SLAVERY ABOLISHED IN CUBA

Slavery in Cuba was abolished by royal decree today in 1886. More than a million West African slaves had been brought to Cuba as part of the Atlantic slave trade to work on the lucrative sugarcane plantations. They vastly outnumbered the European population, and today perhaps as many as 60 percent of Cubans are descended from these African slaves. We're celebrating the beginning of the end of a terrible era with a Cuba Libre.

Teddy Beartini

1½ shots pear cognac liqueur
¾ shot apple schnapps liqueur
1½ shots apple juice
1 pinch cinnamon

Shake ingredients with ice and strain into chilled glass. Garnish with pear slice.

BRING YOUR TEDDY BEAR TO WORK DAY

If you've picked up this book too late today to take your teddy bear to work, we suggest you make it up to him now by mixing a Teddy Bear 'Tini and snuggling up for the rest of the evening on the sofa together.

Che's Revolution

4 fresh mint leaves • 2 shots light white rum • 2 shots pineapple juice • ¼ shot maple syrup

Muddle mint with rum in base of shaker. Add other ingredients, shake with ice and strain into chilled glass. Garnish with pineapple wedge.

CHE GUEVARA DIES

On this day in 1967, Bolivian paramilitaries, working with the CIA, executed Che Guevara, and spawned a thousand T-shirts. Although famed and demonized in equal measure for his role in the Cuban revolution, Ernesto Guevara was, in fact, not Cuban but Argentinian. He was a medical student when he set out on an epic road trip across Latin America, which he would immortalize in his book *The Motorcycle Diaries*. The injustices he witnessed on his travels—from lepers to exploited workers—left him believing that violent revolution was the only way forward. More than half a century later, Che is still a hero to many—Cuban schoolchildren promise to be like him—and a demon to others. Today, we're drinking to his memory with a Che's Revolution.

Arizona Breeze

2½ shots London dry gin • 3 shots cranberry juice • 2 shots pink grapefruit juice

Shake ingredients with ice and strain into ice-filled glass. Garnish with grapefruit wedge.

LONDON BRIDGE MOVES TO ARIZONA

In 1971 today the town of Lake Havasu City in Arizona debuted a new bridge: London Bridge. When it had become too weak to carry the volume of London traffic required, Arizonan entrepreneur Robert P. McCulloch bought the bridge, for almost two and a half million dollars. He then shipped the individually numbered stones from the dismantled bridge out to Arizona and rebuilt London Bridge over a local canal, a project that took four years to complete. Visitors can now enjoy a ninety-minute tour of the bridge, taking in the strafing scars from World War II. It is second only to the Grand Canyon as a tourist attraction in Arizona. Today we are toasting the state that now hosts a British bridge with an Arizona Breeze.

Mai Tai

*2 shots aged rum • ½ shot orange curaçao liqueur • ¾ shot lime juice
¼ shot almond (orgeat) syrup • ¼ shot sugar syrup*

Shake ingredients with ice and strain into glass filled with crushed ice. Garnish with lime wedge, pineapple cube, maraschino cherry and mint.

A BARTENDING LEGEND LEAVES US

Gentleman bartender and gentleman scoundrel, one-legged rumormonger and foulmouthed tiki deity, Victor Bergeron died on this day in 1984—and a legend died with him. "Trader Vic" was eighty-one and missed the fiftieth anniversary of his business empire by a matter of weeks—he had started Hinky Dink's on November 17, 1934. Vic once claimed that he'd do anything to get customers, including sticking an ice pick in his wooden leg, and his feud with Donn Beach is a bartending legend. Yet he was also a sculptor, a painter, a jewelry designer, a fossil geek and an apostle of rum in all its marvelous variations. Trader Vic, we salute you. We are toasting you with a Mai Tai—your own, of course.

Sangria Martini

*1 shot Shiraz red wine • 1½ shots Cognac V.S.O.P. • ¾ shot orange juice
½ shot apple schnapps liqueur • ½ shot crème de framboise liqueur*

Shake ingredients with ice and strain into chilled glass. Garnish with orange slice.

NATIONAL DAY IN SPAIN

Today is a holiday in Spain as the country celebrates its national day: the Fiesta Nacional de España. Why today? Well, bizarrely enough, today is the day that Christopher Columbus arrived in the Americas. Although Columbus himself was an Italian from Genoa, he claimed the Americas for his Spanish employers, so today is also a chance for Spaniards to celebrate their common Hispanic heritage with inhabitants of their former empires overseas. We'll be marking the occasion with a Sangria Martini, a slightly more adult yet extremely moreish take on the ancient Spanish blend that has become a classic.

Noon

1½ shots London dry gin • ¾ shot dry vermouth • ¾ shot sweet vermouth
¾ shot orange juice • 2 dashes bitters • ½ fresh egg white

Shake ingredients with ice and strain into chilled glass. Garnish with orange zest twist.

GREENWICH MEAN TIME ESTABLISHED

From this day in 1884, following a lengthy conference convened by the United States, noon in London's Greenwich Observatory set the time zones for the rest of the world, and the thin line that runs through the building came to mark the division between east and west. Until then, nations had been drawing maps with zero degrees longitude at different points, making mapping and navigation incredibly difficult. Different maps placed the dividing line between east and west in Jerusalem, Oslo, Paris, Rome, Pisa, Copenhagen, Philadelphia, Washington, the Canary Islands and more. The day gives us a rather marvelous excuse to drink an aptly named Noon cocktail and also to remember the dying art of chart navigation.

Abbey Martini

2 shots London dry gin • 1 shot sweet vermouth • 1 shot orange juice • 3 dashes bitters

Shake ingredients with ice and strain into chilled glass. Garnish with orange zest twist.

ENGLAND DEFEATED BY FRANCE

Duke William II of Normandy had spent nine months building a fleet large enough to cross the channel and invade England, and it was on this day in 1066 that he met with the English army under the Anglo-Saxon King Harold II about seven miles in from the English coast, close to the present-day town of Battle in East Sussex. It was a decisive Norman victory, which sealed William's conquest of England. Estimates suggest that two thousand invaders died along with about twice that number of Englishmen. William is said to have founded a monastery on the site of the battle, with the high altar of the abbey church at the spot where King Harold died, so today we will be drinking an Abbey Martini.

Dark 'n' Stormy

2 shots dark rum • 1 shot lime juice • ½ shot sugar syrup • top with ginger beer

Shake first three ingredients with ice and strain into ice-filled glass. Top with ginger beer and stir.
Garnish with lime wedge.

BRITAIN'S SECOND GREAT STORM

Some fifteen million trees were downed today in 1987 during the worst storm Britain had known since the Great Storm of 1703. Despite the gathering winds, BBC weather forecaster Michael Fish famously brushed the threat aside with the now notorious remark, "Earlier on today, apparently, a woman rang the BBC and said she'd heard there was a hurricane on the way...well, if you're watching, don't worry, there isn't!" Technically the second Great Storm wasn't a hurricane. Winds reached hurricane force (12 on the Beaufort Scale), but because the weather system hadn't come from the tropics, it didn't count as a hurricane. It was, however, a pretty extreme piece of weather. We are raising a glass to poor Michael Fish with an aptly named Dark 'n' Stormy.

Dorian Gray

1½ shots light white rum • ¾ shot Grand Marnier • 1 shot orange juice • ¾ shot cranberry juice.

Shake ingredients with ice and strain into chilled glass. Garnish with orange zest twist.

OSCAR WILDE'S BIRTHDAY

Son of a knighted surgeon and his artistic wife, Oscar Wilde was born on this day in 1854 in Dublin, Ireland. He'd go on to craft novels, plays and poems and ultimately scandalize the world. Wilde was also an absinthe fan. He observed that "a glass of absinthe is as poetical as anything in the world" and went on to describe the intoxicating effects of the Green Fairy. After a first stage of ordinary drunkenness, Wilde said, you enter the first stage of hallucination, where you see "monstrous and cruel things," and then the second stage, "where you see things that you want to see." Today we are toasting one of literature's greatest wits with a Dorian Gray, named for Oscar Wilde's most notorious literary creation.

Jack Pot

½ shot Drambuie • ¼ shot blended scotch whisky • ¼ shot Islay whisky
¼ shot Irish whiskey • ¼ shot Welsh single malt whiskey • ¾ shot London dry gin
1½ shots British bitter ale • ¼ shot apple juice

Stir ingredients with ice and strain into chilled glass. Garnish with strawberry and mint.

THE LONDON BEER FLOOD

This day in 1814 was very lucky for a handful of Londoners (though sadly rather unlucky for others) when a twenty-three-foot-tall vat holding more than 160,000 gallons of beer ruptured, causing other gigantic vats in the same brewery to do the same. As the tidal wave of beer flooded the streets around present-day Tottenham Court Road, people raced onto the streets to scoop up as much as they could. Sadly the force of the wave destroyed two houses and a pub, and at least eight people drowned in flooded basements. The brewery was taken to court, but the judge and jury declared the disaster an act of God. The day has inspired us to drink a Jack Pot, with its hint of London Bitter.

Black Tie

1 shot aged rum • ½ shot light white rum • ½ shot triple sec • ¼ shot almond (orgeat) syrup
½ teaspoon blackstrap molasses • ¾ shot lime juice • ⅛ shot sugar syrup

Shake ingredients with ice and strain into ice-filled glass. Garnish with cape gooseberry.

CRAVAT DAY

By order of the Croatian parliament, today is Cravat Day, a chance to celebrate the humble tie and practice Croat pride—for, unless you believe the Iranians, both the word *cravat* and the necktie that it denotes come from Croatia. Legend relates that it was Croatian mercenaries who exported red neckties to the rest of Europe in the 17th century, by way of the famously dapper King Louis XIV of France, but it was definitely Croats who on today's date in 2003 tied the largest tie in the world around a Roman arena—the knot alone was 161 feet wide—and it was Croats who equipped a medieval bell tower with a red tie. Today, statues across Zagreb will be dressed up in red ties, so why not wear a tie to work and join us in a Black Tie Cocktail?

Black Rose

1 shot bourbon whiskey
1 shot Cognac V.S.O.P.
¼ shot pomegranate (grenadine) syrup
3 dashes Peychaud's Bitters
1 dash bitters

Stir ingredients with ice and strain into chilled empty glass. Garnish with lemon zest twist.

BLACK MONDAY

On Black Monday, October 19, 1987, when the world's stock markets crashed, the Dow Jones dropped by what is still the greatest percentage loss of all time: more than 22 percent. By the end of the month, the Hong Kong stock market had almost halved in value, Australia's was down more than 40 percent and British stocks were worth less than three-quarters of what they had been two weeks before. In case this memory is too much, we suggest a Black Rose, a soft, Sazerac-style cocktail that should take the edge off most financial anxieties.

Waltzing Matilda

1 fresh passion fruit • 1 shot London dry gin • 2 shots sauvignon blanc wine
⅛ shot Grand Marnier
top with ginger ale

Cut passion fruit in half and scoop out flesh into shaker. Add next three ingredients, shake with ice and strain into ice-filled glass. Top with ginger ale.

SYDNEY OPERA HOUSE OPENS

One of the 20th century's architectural icons was unveiled to the world on this day in 1973 when the queen opened the Sydney Opera House. It had taken more than sixteen years to build, phenomenal engineering innovations, some notorious political infighting and even street demonstrations across the city when the original architect resigned in 1966. Because Sydney wouldn't be the same without the opera house, we're marking the opening of this great building with a musically named and very Australian Waltzing Matilda.

Nelson's Blood

1½ shots Cognac V.S.O.P.
1½ shots ruby port

Stir ingredients with ice and strain into chilled glass. Garnish with lemon zest twist.

DEATH OF NELSON

As Napoleon massed his forces on the French coast ready to invade Britain, the British fleet gathered just west of Spain's Cape Trafalgar, ready to take on the French and Spanish navies. The battle took place on this day in 1805 and, thanks to Lord Nelson, victory went to the British. Sadly, though, Nelson gave his life during the battle, his spine shattered by a bullet. Legend has it that his body was brought home in rum, giving the spirit its nickname, Nelson's Blood, so the thoroughly rummy Nelson's Blood cocktail makes an eminently suitable memorial.

Texsun

1½ shots bourbon whiskey • 1½ shots dry vermouth • 1½ shots pink grapefruit juice

Shake ingredients with ice and strain into chilled glass. Garnish with lemon zest twist.

TEXAS ELECTS ITS FIRST PRESIDENT

Today in 1836 Sam Houston became the first elected president of the Republic of Texas, which had declared its independence from Mexico a year previously and officially formed the Republic of Texas in March 1836. Texas is one of the very few states to have been an independent country. Its existence sprang from a revolution in the Mexican state of Coahuila y Tejas, where citizens objected (among other things) to having to adopt Catholicism. The Texas revolution had lasted for a year, but Mexico didn't recognize its independence, and conflicts continued for a further decade or so—pretty much until Texas gave up its independence and joined the United States, officially becoming the state of Texas in 1846. Today, we'll be raising a glass to Texas, and Texans, with a Texsun cocktail.

Zhivago

1½ shots vanilla-infused vodka • ½ shot bourbon whiskey • ½ shot sour apple liqueur
1 shot lime juice • ¾ shot sugar syrup

Shake ingredients with ice and strain into chilled glass. Garnish with apple slice.

BORIS PASTERNAK WINS A NOBEL PRIZE

Boris Pasternak spent his literary career walking a fine line with Soviet authorities and published *Doctor Zhivago* at great personal risk. When on this day in 1958 the Nobel Committee awarded him the Nobel Prize for Literature, he was informed by Soviet authorities that if he went to Stockholm to receive his medal, he would be refused re-entry to the Soviet Union. Pasternak felt obliged to telegraph the Nobel Committee, "In view of the meaning given the award by the society in which I live, I must renounce this undeserved distinction." As a defender of freedom, Pasternak found it one of the toughest decisions of his life and he was later criticized for it by Aleksandr Solzhenitsyn. Today we are remembering Boris Pasternak and his great novel with a Zhivago cocktail.

Golden Dream

1 shot triple sec
1 shot Galliano L'Autentico liqueur
2 shots orange juice
1 shot whipping cream

Shake ingredients with ice and strain into chilled glass. Serve with ladyfinger.

UNITED NATIONS DAY

On this day in 1945, as the world struggled to cope with the aftermath of World War II and the strange new world order, the United Nations came into being with the goal of preventing such a dreadful conflict from ever happening again. Today, 193 nations belong to the United Nations. We'll be drinking to this important aspiration with a Golden Dream and hoping for world peace.

Pilgrim

1½ shots golden rum • ½ shot Grand Marnier • 1 shot orange juice
¾ shot lime juice • ¼ shot pimento allspice liqueur • 3 dashes bitters

Shake ingredients with ice and strain into chilled glass. Garnish with freshly grated nutmeg.

CHAUCER DIED ON THIS DAY

Geoffrey Chaucer was crucial in establishing the legitimacy of vernacular, Middle English, when the dominant literary languages at the time in England were French and Latin. Widely considered the greatest English poet of the Middle Ages, and most famously known for his *Canterbury Tales*, on this day in 1400 Chaucer became the first poet to be buried in Poet's Corner in Westminster Abbey. *The Canterbury Tales* differs from other literature of the period in terms of its naturalism, its varied characters and the variety of stories the pilgrims tell. Today we are toasting this great work with a Pilgrim cocktail.

Tanglefoot

2 shots light white rum • 1 shot Swedish punch liqueur • ½ shot lemon juice
½ shot orange juice

Shake ingredients with ice and strain into chilled glass. Garnish with orange zest twist.

FOUNDING OF THE U.K. FOOTBALL ASSOCIATION

Before the first meeting of the Football Association in the Freemasons' Tavern in Great Queen Street, London, today in 1863, there were no nationally recognized football (soccer) rules. The game was played in schools to local guidelines, but when boys from different regions met, mayhem descended, so the Football Association (now the oldest football association in the world) was formed to agree to a set of rules. It's quite fun to think of the players jumbled up on the pitch with no common rules, so today we're drinking to that memory, and to the FA for sorting it all out, with a Tanglefoot.

Bacardi Cocktail

2 shots light white rum • ½ shot lime juice • ¼ shot pomegranate (grenadine) syrup
½ shot cold water • ⅛ shot sugar syrup

Shake ingredients with ice and strain into chilled glass. Garnish with maraschino cherry.

ST. VINCENT AND THE GRENADINES' INDEPENDENCE DAY

Today is party time in St. Vincent and the Grenadines, one of the world's smaller—though by no means its smallest—nations. These West Indian islands will be celebrating their independence from Great Britain, achieved in 1979, with steel drums, calypso, soca, reggae and, of course, rum. We are taking the opportunity to enjoy a classic Bacardi Cocktail, created in Cuba in 1917. In 1938 a court ruled that "Bacardi Rum is unique and uncopyable" and issued a ruling that a Bacardi Cocktail must legally be made with rum manufactured by the Compañia Ron Bacardi.

Rum Runner

1½ shots navy rum • ½ shot crème de mûre • 1 shot crème de banane liqueur • 1 shot lime juice
2 shots pineapple juice • ½ shot pomegranate (grenadine) syrup

Shake ingredients with ice and strain into glass filled with crushed ice. Garnish with pineapple wedge and maraschino cherry.

PROHIBITION ACT PASSED

Congress voted the 18th Amendment to the Constitution, otherwise known as the Volstead Act, or the National Prohibition Act, into law on this day in 1919, but Prohibition proved to be an infamous failure. The first documented breach of the new law occurred at 12:59 AM on January 17, 1920, just under an hour after it came into effect, when armed men stole a massive quantity of allegedly "medicinal" whiskey from a train. Things went, pretty much, downhill from there, launching the careers of such celebrated gangsters as Al Capone. Today's cocktail, a Rum Runner, recalls all those bootleggers who kept running liquor illegally into the country and across state borders.

Black Martini

1½ shots light white rum • 1½ shots dark crème de cacao liqueur • 1½ shots espresso coffee

Shake ingredients with ice and strain into chilled glass. Garnish with grated white chocolate.

ANNIVERSARY OF THE WALL STREET CRASH

On this day, which was to become known as Black Tuesday, in 1929, the stock market lost more than $14 billion in a single day, an event that most historians consider marks the beginning of the Great Depression. Did Wall Street's finest leap from their windows, as many believe? Not as many as you would think. Though Winston Churchill witnessed a suicide in New York the day after Black Tuesday, one man who was dragged from a window ledge before he could jump turned out to be a window cleaner. While some of the city's great and good did turn to suicide in the aftermath of the crash, it's likely that many more turned to a restorative drink. We think a Black Martini would have been a good option.

Gloom Lifter

1½ shots Irish whiskey • ½ shot Cognac V.S.O.P. • ⅓ shot pomegranate (grenadine) syrup
1 shot lemon juice • ¼ shot sugar syrup • ½ fresh egg white

Dry shake ingredients. Shake again with ice and strain into chilled glass. Garnish with lemon wedge.

CREATE A GREAT FUNERAL DAY

Don't leave it until the last minute, or even too late altogether, but seize the day today, save your relatives the heartache and plan your own funeral now. Yes, this is a real day on the annual calendar and it was created in 1999 to get people talking about their own funeral. After having what might not be the cheeriest conversation of your life, we suggest you brighten things up with a Gloom Lifter.

Bitches' Brew

1 shot rhum agricole
1 shot aged rum
1 shot lime juice
½ shot pimento allspice liqueur
½ shot sugar syrup
1 shot egg (white and yolk)

Dry shake ingredients. Add ice, shake again and strain
into chilled glass. Garnish with grated nutmeg.

HALLOWEEN

Traditionally, Halloween is the eve of the western Christian feast of All Hallows' Day, which is dedicated to remembering the dead, including saints (the hallows) and departed believers. Indeed, in some parts of the world, the Christian observances of All Hallows' Eve include large gatherings in cemeteries to light candles on the graves of the dead. Many of today's Halloween customs are thought to have evolved from the early folk customs and beliefs of Celtic-speaking countries, some of which have pagan roots. Since 1974, New York City's Greenwich Village has hosted the world's largest Halloween parade. It stretches over a mile and includes more than sixty thousand costumed participants, circus performers, floats, live bands and giant puppets. Tonight we're not mixing a witch's brew but a Bitches' Brew, a Flip-style concoction that's easy to prepare in batches, too, so if you're throwing a party tonight, this is a useful recipe.

November

Angel's Share

1 teaspoon marmalade
2 shots Cognac V.S.O.P.
¼ shot Licor 43
½ shot lemon juice
¼ shot sugar syrup

Stir heaped spoon of orange marmalade with cognac in base of shaker until marmalade dissolves. Add other ingredients, shake with ice and strain into chilled glass. Garnish with orange zest twist.

SISTINE CHAPEL REVELATION

On this day, the Feast of All Saints, in 1512, Pope Julius II inaugurated the Vatican's Sistine Chapel with a solemn Mass and revealed Michelangelo's magnificent artwork. Michelangelo found the four years of work so hard that he wrote a poem complaining about the "torture" involved. He must therefore have been a glutton for punishment, as he returned more than twenty years later to create his iconic *Last Judgment*. Today more than five million visitors a year visit the chapel to admire Michelangelo's art, and cardinals still gather there to elect a new pope. The Angel's Share cocktail that we are drinking tonight in honor of Michelangelo is based on cognac, one of many spirits from which the angels are said to take their share (through evaporation) as it ages.

Oaxaca Old-Fashioned

1½ shots tequila
½ shot mezcal
1 teaspoon agave syrup
1 dash bitters

Stir tequila with three ice cubes in a glass. Add other ingredients and stir with more ice. Top with ice and stir some more. Garnish with orange zest twist.

DAY OF THE DEAD

Today is the Feast of All Souls in the Catholic Church, and the Day of the Dead (Día de los Muertos) in Mexico, an occasion that seamlessly blends Christian beliefs with rituals so ancient that the Aztecs would probably recognize them. Families reunite to tend their ancestors' graves and honor them with offerings including flowers, food and little sugar skulls, in place of the real ones the Aztecs might have donated, and, of course, drink. Ancestors seem to favor bottles of pulque, tequila, mezcal or the porridgelike corn drink known as atole. Get in the spirit by mixing up an Oaxaca Old-Fashioned, named for the southern Mexican city that's particularly famous for its Day of the Dead celebrations. Based on tequila with a hint of smoky mezcal, it showcases not one but two indigenous Mexican liquors.

Larchmont

*1½ shots light white rum • ½ shot Grand Marnier • ½ shot lime juice
¼ shot sugar syrup • ½ shot cold water*

Shake ingredients with ice and strain into chilled glass. Garnish with orange zest twist.

THE FINE ART OF DAVID EMBURY

Thanks to author David A. Embury's extensive knowledge of the history of cocktails, his theories of flavor and his lucid, almost scientific approach to drink, his book *The Fine Art of Mixing Drinks* is recognized as a seminal work on cocktails. A Manhattan-based tax attorney, Embury was born on this day in 1886 in Pine Woods, upstate New York. He was a sociable, clubbable man whose career success was partly due to his ability to draw in new clientele. Embury's 1948 volume would become a bible for 1950s middle-class entertaining and is a vital resource for professional bartenders today. Remember him with a Larchmont, a delicate orange Daiquiri cocktail that he named for the Westchester County village in which he lived.

Dream Cocktail

1½ shots Cognac V.S.O.P. • ¾ shot triple sec • ⅛ shot anisette liqueur • ½ shot cold water

Shake ingredients with ice and strain into chilled glass. Garnish with lemon zest twist.

FREUD'S WISH FULFILLED

Today in 1899 a little-known Austrian neurologist named Sigmund Freud published *The Interpretation of Dreams*. It would take many years before that first 600-copy print run sold out, yet the publication would go on to inspire the Surrealists and transform our understanding of the human mind by suggesting that dreams reflect the hidden desires and anxieties of the subconscious. Once the anxieties of the subconscious were cured, Freud believed men could be happier. In honor of Freud, the father of psychoanalysis, who transformed mental-health treatment with his talking cure but sadly had to flee his Vienna home to escape Nazism for London in old age, mix up a Dream Cocktail tonight. Aniseed, orange and cognac make a positively dreamy after-dinner combo.

Hot Buttered Rum

2 teaspoons runny honey
1 pat butter
2 shots golden rum
1 dash nutmeg
top with boiling water

Place teaspoon loaded with honey in warmed glass. Add other ingredients and stir until honey and butter are dissolved. Garnish with cinnamon stick and lemon slice studded with cloves.

BONFIRE NIGHT

An old British children's rhyme begins, "Remember, remember the Fifth of November, gunpowder, treason and plot." Around the time that Hindu cultures hold Diwali, their festival of light, Britons light up the sky with fireworks in memory of an early religious terrorist, Guy Fawkes. A Catholic, Guy Fawkes was arrested while trying to blow up the Houses of Parliament around midnight on November 4, 1605. The plan was to eliminate the Protestant King James I and the country's political elite, then lead a rebellion to restore a Catholic regime. Fawkes was condemned to death as a traitor and died horribly, leaping from the scaffold to avoid a traitor's death. Today, Britons remember his treachery with bonfires, processions and the burning of effigies. If you're hosting a fireworks party tonight, an ancient toddy, the Hot Buttered Rum, makes an outstanding choice to enjoy by the fireside.

Swedish Ale Punch

2 shots bourbon whiskey
1 shot Swedish punch liqueur
1 shot pink grapefruit juice
top with British bitter ale

Shake first three ingredients with ice and strain into chilled glass. Top with beer. Garnish with grapefruit slice.

GUSTAVUS ADOLPHUS DAY

Between taking the throne of Sweden at the age of just sixteen and dying in battle today in 1632, Gustavus Adolphus the Great transformed his nation from a little-known country to a major player on the European scene. The military theorist Clausewitz listed him alongside Alexander the Great and Napoleon as one of the greatest generals of all time. Today Swedes, and people of Swedish heritage elsewhere in the world, commemorate his legacy, both as a general and as an educator. Why not join in the fun, with a Swedish Ale Punch, based on bourbon, beer and Sweden's national liqueur, Swedish Punsch?

Champs-Elysées

1¾ shots Cognac V.S.O.P. • ¼ shot green Chartreuse • ½ shot lemon juice
½ shot sugar syrup • 3 dashes bitters
¾ shot cold water • ½ fresh egg white

Shake ingredients with ice and strain into chilled glass. Garnish with lemon zest twist.

REMEMBER SCIENCE'S FIRST LADY

The first woman to become a professor at the University of Paris, the first woman to win a Nobel Prize, the first person to win two Nobel Prizes and the first independent woman to be entombed in Paris's famous Panthéon, Marie Skłodowska-Curie was born in Warsaw, Poland, on this day in 1867. During her career she discovered two elements, radium and polonium, pioneered the study of the atom, founded a science dynasty and drove ambulances among the trenches of World War I. Remember this Franco–Polish citizen of the world with a Champs-Elysées, a cognac creation named for her adopted home, Paris.

Harvey Wallbanger

2 shots vodka
½ shot Galliano L'Autentico liqueur
3½ shots orange juice

Pour ingredients into ice-filled glass. Garnish with orange zest twist.

HARVEY WALLBANGER DAY

Of all the cocktails to have its very own day, the Harvey Wallbanger is probably the most surprising. But, yes, Harvey Wallbanger Day is a thing. Further, Harvey Wallbanger Cake is a thing, too. A much-maligned 1960s favorite, the Harvey Wallbanger comes a little before the Sex on the Beach, the Woo Woo and the Snowball on many veteran bartenders' lists of drinks they least like to serve. Made with freshly squeezed orange juice, however, the herbal flavors of Galliano sing. So break out the juicer, dust off that Galliano and surprise yourself with a Harvey Wallbanger tonight.

Berlin Sour

2 shots kümmel • ½ shot maraschino liqueur • 1 shot lemon juice • ¼ shot sugar syrup

Shake ingredients with ice and strain into chilled glass. Garnish with lemon slice and maraschino cherry.

BERLIN WALL TOPPLED

On this day in 1989, protestors tore down the Berlin Wall, which had divided communist East Germany from capitalist West Germany since 1961. The wall was a potent symbol of communist power and audiences around the world watched in awe as people dismantled it, slab by slab—some entrepreneurial types saving pieces to sell as souvenirs. The end of the wall was a great moment for Germany, a great moment for the world, and a signal that a new era was beginning, as the Iron Curtain that had divided Europe fell, live on international TV. Commemorate this amazing day with a Berlin Sour, invented in Frankfurt and enriched with the caraway-cumin spice of that Central European favorite, kümmel liqueur.

Irish Coffee

1⅓ oz. whipping cream • 1½ shots Irish whiskey • ½ shot muscovado sugar syrup • 2½ oz. hot filter coffee

Warm a heatproof glass. Lightly whip cream. Pour whiskey, sugar syrup and hot coffee into warmed glass until it is about three-quarters full and stir. Float whipped cream by pouring over the back of a warmed spoon.

IRISH COFFEE COMES TO AMERICA

The splendidly named Stanton Delaplane, a columnist for the *San Francisco Chronicle*, may have won a Pulitzer Prize for Reporting, but his legacy remains that icon of 1960s sophistication, the Irish Coffee. On this day in 1952, Stanton sat with Jack Koeppler, then owner of San Francisco's Buena Vista café, trying to re-create a drink he'd discovered in Dublin airport: the Irish Coffee. It would take a while before Koeppler perfected the recipe pioneered by Ireland's Joe Sheridan, yet once he did a global phenomenon was born. Stanton himself gave up drinking within five years, but the Buena Vista still churns out thousands every day. So put aside your preconceptions, warm a glass and some cream, and enjoy this classic coffee cocktail tonight.

Fallen Leaves

1½ shots calvados
1½ shots sweet vermouth
½ shot dry vermouth
¼ shot Cognac V.S.O.P

Stir ingredients with ice and strain into chilled glass.
Garnish with lemon zest twist.

FIRST GLOBAL CONFLICT ENDS

Today is Veterans Day, which is Remembrance Day across the Commonwealth and Armistice Day in France and Belgium—a solemn occasion when we remember the men and women who fell during World War I, as well as those who have served or lost their lives in wars since then. It was on the 11th hour of the 11th day of the 11th month of 1918 that World War I hostilities formally ended. Yet, insanely, some generals still threw soldiers into action even after the armistice had been signed—the last casualty of the war, Baltimore's Henry Gunther, died just one minute before the scheduled start of peace. Today is a somber anniversary, that's for sure, but an important one: we recommend you commemorate it with Charles Schumann's calvados-based creation, the suitably solemn Fallen Leaves.

Bramble

2 shots London dry gin • 1 shot lemon juice • ½ shot sugar syrup • ½ shot crème de mûre

Shake first three ingredients with ice and strain into glass filled with crushed ice. Drizzle liqueur over drink to create a "bleeding" effect in the glass. Garnish with blackberries and lemon slice.

WORLD WIDE WEB'S BIRTHDAY

When London-born computer scientist Tim Berners-Lee sent out a memo entitled "WorldWideWeb: Proposal for a HyperText Project" on this day in 1990, he reckoned it would take five people working for six months, with a software and hardware budget of around £80,000, to complete. The project he proposed, a space where all users could create, share and expand knowledge, has transformed the world at least as dramatically as the printing press did, democratizing knowledge on a level that has never before been seen. Berners-Lee's memo outlined HTML (HyperText Markup Language), the linking glue that binds the Internet together, and so we think it's appropriate to celebrate with a true British cocktail named for the ultimate binding plant—Dick Bradsell's 20th-century classic, the Bramble.

Martinez

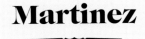

2 shots Old Tom gin • ¼ shot dry vermouth • ¾ shot sweet vermouth
¼ shot maraschino liqueur • 1 dash bitters

Stir ingredients with ice and strain into chilled glass. Garnish with orange zest twist.

MARTINI FANATIC DEPARTS

You can no more keep a martini in the refrigerator than you can keep a kiss there. The proper union of gin and vermouth is a great and sudden glory; it is one of the happiest marriages on earth and one of the shortest-lived." Academic, journalist, novelist and bard of (some) American cocktails, Bernard DeVoto died today in 1955, leaving behind one of the most cantankerous yet wonderfully written tributes to the cocktail ever: *The Hour: A Cocktail Manifesto*. Despite his abuse of the Manhattan as an abomination, the man's praise for the Martini wins our vote. We are toasting him with what's probably its ancestor, the Martinez, in our favorite variation, with old-school Old Tom gin.

Indian Rose

2½ shots London dry gin
¼ shot apricot brandy liqueur
¼ shot rose water
¼ shot rose syrup
½ shot cold water

Shake ingredients with ice and strain into chilled glass. Garnish with rose petal.

CHILDREN'S DAY IN INDIA

While much of the world celebrates Children's Day in June, India has chosen today to honor its youth. Why? Well, Jawaharlal Nehru, the first prime minister of India, was born on this day in 1889. After fighting for Indian independence under Gandhi, Nehru ruled India from its establishment as its own nation in 1947 until his death in 1964. Indian children remember him today as Chacha Nehru (Uncle Nehru) and praise his lifelong passion and work for the welfare, education and development of children and young people. Toast Nehru and India's future with an Indian Rose.

Creamy Vanilla Colada

2 shots aged rum
1½ shots yogurt liqueur
6 drops vanilla extract

Shake ingredients with ice and strain into chilled glass. Garnish with cocoa powder.

TIME FOR A SMOOTH, CLOSE SHAVE

The fabulously named King Camp Gillette patented a new kind of razor on this day in 1904, putting countless barbershops out of business and making shaving rather safer than it had been in the days of cutthroat razors and the demon barber Sweeney Todd. It took the Wisconsin-born eccentric two years to produce steel that was hard, thin and cheap enough to make safe disposable blades—but he did, and his company was sold for more than fifty billion dollars in 2005. Celebrate close shaves and soft jawlines tonight with a supersmooth Creamy Vanilla Colada.

Havanatheone

10 fresh mint leaves • 2 shots light white rum • 2 teaspoons runny honey
½ shot lime juice • 1 shot apple juice

Lightly muddle mint (just to bruise) in base of shaker. Add rum and honey and stir until honey dissolves. Add other ingredients, shake with ice and strain into chilled glass. Garnish with mint.

HAPPY BIRTHDAY, HAVANA

Today is Havana's birthday, an occasion that its residents commemorate by walking around the ceiba tree next to El Templete, a shrine placed on the spot where Spanish colonists first said Mass on this day in 1519. Founded as San Cristóbal de La Habana in a natural bay, the city is today the capital of Cuba and home to around four million people. It is also the epicenter of a vibrant cocktail culture that expanded and exploded thanks to the activities of the *cantineros* (bartenders) during Prohibition. Why not drink to Havana with a Havanatheone, a floral, fruity take on the island's iconic Daiquiri?

Casino

1½ shots London dry gin
¾ shot maraschino liqueur
½ shot lemon juice • ¼ shot cold water
1 dash orange bitters

Shake ingredients with ice and strain into chilled glass. Garnish with maraschino cherry.

DIRECTOR BREAKS NEW GROUND

One of the world's most influential directors, the man behind *Goodfellas, Raging Bull, The Last Temptation of Christ, The Wolf of Wall Street* and, of course, *Casino*, was born in Queens, New York City, on this day in 1942. A onetime altar boy, Martin Scorsese entered a seminary to train for the priesthood before starting his movie career. He directed Michael Jackson's iconic *Bad*, worked with Robert De Niro on at least eight films and is, of course, the subject of a charming ode by art-rockers King Missile. We are sipping a citrusy Casino in his honor.

Mint Julep

12 fresh mint leaves
2½ shots bourbon whiskey
¾ shot sugar syrup
3 dashes bitters

Shake ingredients with ice, strain into julep cup filled with crushed ice and stir. Garnish with lemon slice and mint dusted with confectioner's sugar.

MICKEY MOUSE'S BIRTHDAY

On November 18, 1928, Walt Disney released a cartoon called *Steamboat Willie*, featuring a character named Mickey Mouse. Though this was not Mickey's first big-screen outing, Disney World Florida celebrates the little mouse's birthday on this day. It's hard to imagine Florida without Mickey. So we're toasting Minnie's beloved with a minty thing, that classic of the Southern states, a Mint Julep, first described by Charles Joseph Latrobe of the Anti-Temperance Society in Saratoga, Florida, back in 1833.

Made Man

1½ shots rye whiskey
¼ shot yellow Chartreuse • ¼ shot cherry brandy liqueur • ⅛ shot Fernet Branca
½ shot cold water

Stir ingredients with ice and strain into chilled glass. Garnish with lemon zest twist.

INTERNATIONAL MEN'S DAY

Since the 1960s, there have been plenty of women's days around the world, but not so many for the men. So International Men's Day, which falls on this day every year, is an occasion to redress the gender balance and honor positive male role models, while raising money for men's health charities and the like. It's also a great chance for anyone who's been growing a 'tache for Movember to get out and about with likeminded guys. Let's raise a toast to all the lovely men in the world with a Made Man and hope it brings them luck and happiness.

Grande Champagne Cosmo

1½ shots Cognac V.S.O.P. • ¾ shot Grand Marnier • ½ shot lemon juice 1 shot cranberry juice • ½ fresh egg white

Shake ingredients with ice and strain into chilled glass. Garnish with orange zest twist.

COSMOS DISCOVERER HITS EARTH

When Edwin Hubble was born in Missouri today in 1889, most people believed that our galaxy, the Milky Way, was the only one in the universe and even that our galaxy *was* the universe. The man who gave his name to the Hubble Space Telescope, which has orbited Earth since 1990, was the first to show that Andromeda, which others considered just stars, was a galaxy, and, further, that our universe was actually expanding. Tonight, toast the discoverer of the cosmos with a Grande Champagne Cosmo, a rich, dark, mind-expanding riff on the 1990s Cosmopolitan.

BBC Cocktail

2 shots aged rum ½ shot Becherovka liqueur 1 dash Wormwood bitters

Stir ingredients with ice and strain into ice-filled glass. Garnish with apple fan.

WORLD TELEVISION DAY

Today is World Television Day, a chance to highlight the role of communications, good and bad, in raising awareness of global issues. Whether you are watching TV tonight or doing something altogether different, we recommend you check out the BBC Cocktail, an intriguing reworking of the classic B & B with the Czech national liquor, Becherovka, in lieu of Bénédictine, and aged rum standing in for brandy. Marian Beke created it during his time at the Artesian Bar in London's Langham Hotel, oft-times off-duty home to the nearby BBC.

Silver Bullet Martini

2 shots London dry gin 1 shot kümmel 1 shot lemon juice ¼ shot sugar syrup

Shake ingredients with ice and strain into chilled glass. Garnish with lemon zest twist.

JFK, RIP

On November 22, 1963, Lee Harvey Oswald assassinated John F. Kennedy, the 35th president of the United States, in Dallas, Texas. The act sent shockwaves around the world—most people who were alive in the 1960s can still recall where they were when they heard the news. And, despite myriad attempts to lay conspiracy theories to rest, competing accounts of what took place can still spark passions more than five decades on. Today we commemorate this sad event with an old kümmel classic, the Silver Bullet Martini.

Egg Nog

2½ shots Cognac V.S.O.P.
½ shot sugar syrup
1 fresh egg (white and yolk)
½ shot whipping cream
2 shots milk
grated nutmeg

Pour ingredients into heatproof glass and stir. Heat in microwave and stir again or mix and warm in pan—do not boil. Garnish with grated nutmeg.

THANKSGIVING

Every fourth Thursday in November, families get together for Thanksgiving— an occasion for turkey, pumpkin pie, lengthy cross-country travel and, of course, eggnog. It was Abraham Lincoln who made Thanksgiving a national occasion, but the tradition goes back to at least 1621, when Puritan colonists in Plymouth, Massachusetts, held a harvest feast to give thanks for a successful growing season. On this occasion the colonists and Native Americans ate together and enjoyed a three-day feast. The colonists provided birds and harvest produce, and the Native Americans killed five deer. If you are celebrating today, why not mix your guests a delicious warming Egg Nog.

Jack-in-the-Box

2 shots calvados
2 shots pineapple juice
2 dashes bitters

Shake ingredients with ice and strain into chilled glass. Garnish with pineapple wedge.

GIN JOINT INTRODUCES JUKEBOX

A San Francisco saloon, the Palais Royale, installed earth's very first jukebox way back on November 23, 1889. That first prototype was not what you'd call communal—it featured four amazingly innovative earpieces attached to a phonograph inside a cabinet. Using one of the earpieces cost five cents, but you didn't get any choice of what to listen to. In the end, the nickel-in-the-slot player really did hit the jackpot, so we are marking today's anniversary with a Jack-in-the-Box as we're guessing a fair number of those early listeners must have got quite a surprise.

Charlie

2 shots bourbon whiskey
½ shot sweet vermouth
¼ shot black raspberry liqueur
1 dash bitters

Stir ingredients with ice and strain into chilled glass. Garnish with maraschino cherry.

DARWIN CHANGES THE WORLD

An English naturalist and geologist who spent almost five years recording the wildlife of Latin America from his base on board the HMS *Beagle*, Charles Darwin published his defining work, *On the Origin of Species*, on this day in 1859. The book, he recorded in his diary, sold out that same day, and the theory of evolution it contained would transform biology, theology, medicine and more. Honor Charles, a courageous man who overcame nervous illness to publish pioneering thought, and his big idea that has shaped our thought, with a Charlie, a pleasantly sweet bourbon confection.

RAC Cocktail

2 shots London dry gin • 1 shot dry vermouth • 1 shot sweet vermouth
⅛ shot pomegranate (grenadine) syrup
1 dash orange bitters

Stir ingredients with ice and strain into chilled glass. Garnish with maraschino cherry.

CAR CREATOR KARL COMES ALONG

Born Karl Friedrich Michael Vaillant in Karlsruhe, Germany, on this day in 1844, Karl Benz would go on to fulfill his lifetime's dream of designing a "horseless carriage," found Mercedes-Benz and invent an engine design still used in some high-performance vehicles today. A child prodigy who went to college at the age of only fifteen, Karl patented his first car, the three-wheeled Patent Motorwagen, in 1886: it was the world's first commercially available automobile. What better way to remember this car pioneer than with the RAC Cocktail, the house cocktail of Britain's Royal Automobile Club? It's a souped-up racer of a Perfect Martini.

Casablanca

2 shots light white rum • ¾ shot triple sec • ¾ shot lime juice
½ shot maraschino liqueur • ½ fresh egg white

Shake ingredients with ice and strain into chilled glass. Garnish with orange zest twist.

CASABLANCA RELEASED

Casablanca, a movie that still routinely tops lists of the best movies of all time, was released on this very day in 1942. The love triangle between cynical bar owner Rick Blaine, "Of all the gin joints in all the towns in all the world, she walks into mine…," played by Humphrey Bogart, his former lover Ilsa Lund (Ingrid Bergman) and her Resistance leader husband Victor Laszlo (Paul Henreid) has aged remarkably well. As befits a movie that received nine Oscar nominations in 1943 and won three statuettes, it has also inspired a number of cocktails. Curl up with a copy of the film and one of our favorite Casablanca cocktails, the Casablanca, a tangy blend of rum, citrus and maraschino. "Play it, Sam."

Divino's

½ shot vodka • 2½ shots Barolo red wine • 1 shot dark crème de cacao liqueur

Shake ingredients with ice and strain into chilled glass. Garnish with grated white chocolate.

DRINKING SONG DEITY DIES

A prolific author of drinking songs—and more delicate poems, too—the Roman poet Horace, the man who brought us *carpe diem* (seize the day), died on this day in 8 BC. Horace also crafted *dulce et decorum est pro patria mori* (it is a sweet and honorable thing to die for one's country), and, most important for us, *nunc est bibendum* (now is the time for drinking). He rose quite phenomenally through Roman society, associating with emperors, generals and politicians despite being the son of a freed slave. Although Horace died before spirits were first produced, we think he would definitely have appreciated this fine combination of vodka, chocolate and wine, discovered in Divino's, Hong Kong.

Kiwi Bellini

1 fresh kiwi fruit • 1¼ shots vodka • ¼ shot lemon juice
¼ shot sugar syrup • top with sparkling wine

Cut kiwi in half, scoop out flesh into base of shaker and muddle. Add next three ingredients, shake with ice and strain into chilled glass. Top with sparkling wine. Garnish with kiwi slice.

WOMEN VOTE FOR THE FIRST TIME

With women now able to vote everywhere but in Saudi Arabia and Vatican City, it's hard to imagine quite what a moment it was when women first trooped to the electoral booths to make their mark. It was New Zealand's women who garnered support from male politicians, and won themselves this right, decades before the U.S. or the U.K. Defying the doom-laden predictions of anti-suffragists, who imagined these delicate Kiwi flowers being jostled and harassed by drunken men, New Zealand women cast their vote in a general election for the first time ever on this day in 1893. We are toasting those brave New Zealand women, and the men whose support was critical to them, with a Kiwi Bellini.

Playmate

1 shot Cognac V.S.O.P. • 1 shot Grand Marnier • 1 shot apricot brandy liqueur
1 shot orange juice • ½ fresh egg white • 3 dashes bitters

Shake ingredients with ice and strain into chilled glass. Garnish with orange zest twist.

GAMING'S BIRTHDAY

Who would have thought three lines and a couple of dots could be so much fun? Pong, the devilishly simple game that kick-started the video-game era, launched on this day in 1962. And this crude variation on table tennis is still an engaging game today, with thousands of unofficial versions and one official one available in the app store. We are not sure whether Atari's designers would even have recognized today's video behemoths, like Destiny, which cost a cool half billion dollars to make in 2014. Yet the birth of a genre is definitely a day to remember—why not do so with a Playmate Martini, which is more sophisticated than its name would suggest?

Atholl Brose

2 teaspoons runny honey
2 shots blended scotch whisky
1½ shots oatmeal water
¼ shot Drambuie
¼ shot amaretto liqueur
½ shot whipping cream

Stir honey with whisky until honey dissolves. Add other ingredients, shake with ice and strain into chilled glass.

(To make the oatmeal water, soak three heaped tablespoons of oatmeal in half a mug of warm water. Stir and leave to stand for fifteen minutes. Strain to extract the creamy liquid and discard what's left of the oatmeal.) Garnish with grated nutmeg.

ST. ANDREW'S DAY

Today is the day when Scots around the world celebrate their patron saint, St. Andrew, who intervened in a memorable battle against the Angles around a thousand years ago. The brother of St. Peter, and an apostle himself, Andrew is, surprisingly, not the patron saint of scotch, or even golf, but of fishermen and Russia. But we still feel it is appropriate to toast him in scotch, as folks of Scottish descent will be doing tonight. Our choice for today is the Atholl Brose, a contemporary take on a very old scotch mix, allegedly named for a Scottish earl of Atholl who crushed a Highland rebellion by filling his opponent's well with the stuff. With oatmeal water, known in its homeland as "brose," plus heather honey, scotch, Drambuie and cream, it couldn't be more Scottish if it were wearing a kilt.

December

Rosarita Margarita

1½ shots tequila • ¾ shot Grand Marnier • ½ shot cranberry juice
½ shot lime cordial • ¾ shot lime juice • ½ shot sugar syrup

Shake ingredients with ice and strain into chilled glass. Garnish with lime wedge and salt rim (optional).

ROSA PARKS RIDES THE BUS

How does a woman become famous for riding a bus? When her name is Rosa Parks. On December 1, 1955, Parks, an African American activist, was sitting in the "colored" section of a bus in segregated Montgomery, Alabama. White people boarded, so the driver moved the "colored" sign down the bus, forcing people with darker skin to stand. When he insisted that Parks give up her seat to people of the shade Alabama law preferred, she refused, was arrested and became the mother of the civil rights movement. An everyday hero and an extraordinary woman, Rosa Parks died at age ninety-one, penniless and facing eviction. Remember her today with a Rosarita Margarita.

Brazilian Nail

1½ shots cachaça • ½ shot blended scotch whisky • ¾ shot Drambuie

Stir ingredients with ice and strain into ice-filled glass. Garnish with orange zest twist.

IN BRAZIL, IT'S SAMBA TIME

If there is one thing more Brazilian than Carnival, it has to be the samba, the rhythm that makes the nation come alive. It should come as no surprise that Brazilians have at least one day of the year dedicated to their national music; remarkably, it is not Mardi Gras but today. It started on this day in 1938 when samba icon Ary Barroso visited the city of Salvador for the very first time—and so today sambistas around the nation will be grooving in his honor. Whether you're beat-deaf or a hip-swinging natural, get into the spirit with a Brazilian Nail. It's a Rusty Nail made even more lovable with a cachaça-shaped dose of Brazilian style.

Smokey Joe

2 shots sake • ½ shot Cognac V.S.O.P. • ¼ shot Islay whisky • 1 shot white dessert wine

Stir ingredients with ice and strain into chilled glass.

HAPPY BIRTHDAY, JOSEPH CONRAD

The man who brought us *Heart of Darkness*, the book that inspired the film *Apocalypse Now*, Joseph Conrad was born in Poland on this day in 1857 and christened Józef Teodor Konrad Korzeniowski. Conrad's early years were spent at sea, exploring the world's farthest corners, and as a born storyteller he later pulled his experiences together to create a body of enduring fiction, thus fulfilling another of his childhood ambitions. Despite growing up Polish and being educated in French, Conrad chose to write in English, a language he only learned in his twenties, because "it's so plastic—if you haven't got a word you need you can make it." As a chain-smoker, we reckon Joseph would have appreciated the peat-smoke richness of our cocktail of the day, the fabulous Smokey Joe.

Z Martini

2½ shots vodka • 1¼ shots tawny port

Stir ingredients with ice and strain into chilled glass. Garnish with olive stuffed with blue cheese

FRANK ZAPPA—IN MEMORIAM

In his 1989 autobiography Frank Zappa famously opined that "you can't be a real country unless you have a beer and an airline." Although notorious for his eccentric behavior, Zappa was actually quite a sophisticated Renaissance man. Musician, composer, film director and wit, he spoke against censorship and inspired musicians from both the rock and classical worlds before his early death on this day in 1993. Garnished with cheese-stuffed olives, the Z Martini has plenty of quirk, though, like the man himself, its port and vodka soul is classical, contemporary and indefinably classy.

Gin Rickey

2 shots gin
½ shot lime juice
¼ shot sugar syrup
top with soda

Shake first three ingredients with ice and strain into ice-filled glass. Top with soda. Garnish wth lime zest twist.

JUST SAY NO!

The "Noble Experiment"—Prohibition—came to an end on this day in 1933, a date now celebrated as Repeal Day. Prohibition had flooded the country with bad booze and worse gangsters, empowered the Mafia and cost the government a fortune in tax revenue. On the flip side, it also brought a grateful nation three great inventions: the booze cruise, first pioneered as a way to drink legally outside U.S. territorial waters; the powder room, a necessity since old-school saloons had no ladies' restrooms; and, of course, the nightclub, which evolved seamlessly from the speakeasy. Better still, as exiled American drinkers and bartenders explored beyond their shores, Prohibition helped drive a bartending revolution that took place as far afield as Italy and Cuba. We are enjoying Repeal Day with a Prohibition favorite that was *The Great Gatsby* author F. Scott Fitzgerald's preferred tipple: the Gin Rickey.

Nicky Finn

1 shot Cognac V.S.O.P.
1 shot triple sec
¼ shot Pernod
1 shot lemon juice

Shake ingredients with ice and strain into chilled glass.
Garnish with lemon zest twist.

ST. NICHOLAS DAY

Happy St. Nicholas Day! The saint best known as Santa Claus died today more than 1,600 years ago, and in many parts of Europe children will wake up to gifts from the man himself this morning. When he's not tending to children, St. Nicholas maintains quite remarkably broad interests—he's the patron saint of brewers, bottlers and wine merchants, not to mention murderers, prisoners, prostitutes and virgins. As Santa Claus, though, he is an invention of 19th-century America—it was American poets, writers and illustrators who transformed the fiery Middle Eastern bishop into the cuddly, red-suited, reindeer-driving man we know today. We are toasting St. Nick with a suitably spiritual concoction, the Nicky Finn, based on cognac, from which both saints and angels take their share.

La Perla

1½ shots tequila • 1½ shots Manzanilla sherry • ¾ shot pear cognac liqueur

Stir ingredients with ice and strain into chilled glass. Garnish with lemon zest twist.

ANNIVERSARY OF PEARL HARBOR

It was today in 1941 that Japanese forces attacked the naval base in Pearl Harbor, Hawaii, killing more than 2,000 Americans and wiping out the bulk of the U.S.'s naval power in the Pacific. Although the country had long been planning for the possibility of war with Japan, no warning of the attack was given, and the traumatized nation was catapulted into global conflict—including, once Hitler declared war on the U.S., the war in Europe. Pearl Harbor was a turning point in world history. We are commemorating it with La Perla, a wonderful tequila blend whose name means, simply, "the pearl."

Benton's Old-Fashioned

2 shots bacon-fat-washed bourbon whiskey* • ¼ shot maple syrup 2 dashes bitters

Stir bourbon and maple syrup in base of mixing glass until syrup dissolves. Add bitters and ice and stir again. Strain into ice-filled glass.

PRETEND TO BE A TIME TRAVELER

Today is your chance to inspect a stranger's smartphone with suspicion and fear as a visitor from the past or to put on your finest futuristic fabrics to summon up a Utopian wonderland. Or simply combine the best of both past and future with the splendidly modern Benton's Old-Fashioned, made with bourbon smoothed by a bacon-fat wash.

*To make the fat-washed bourbon, grill 4 slices of bacon to obtain 1 oz. warm fat. Pour fat into 23½ oz. of bourbon. Infuse for one day before placing bottle in freezer to solidify fat, then clarify the bourbon by straining into a clean bottle. Garnish with orange zest twist.

Coronation Cocktail No. 1

1½ shots fino sherry ¼ shot maraschino liqueur 1½ shots dry vermouth 2 dashes orange bitters

Stir ingredients with ice and strain into chilled glass. Garnish with orange zest twist.

THE BRITISH SOAP THAT RUNS AND RUNS

Ever since the TV series *As the World Turns* finished its epic run in 2010, *Coronation Street* has been the world's longest-running soap opera. The British tale of life in the fictional town of Weatherfield (based on Salford in Greater Manchester) debuted on this day in 1960. Over the decades it has featured guest appearances ranging from Prince Charles to Sir Ian "Gandalf" McKellen, and some of its early stars have worked on the show for more than fifty years. We are toasting its impressive longevity with a Coronation Cocktail No. 1, which includes a terribly British fino sherry.

Gun Club Punch No. 1

1 shot light white rum
1 shot navy rum
1 shot lime juice
1½ shots pineapple juice
¼ shot triple sec
¼ shot pomegranate (grenadine) syrup

Blend ingredients with 12 oz. crushed ice. Garnish with pineapple wedge, maraschino cherry and mint.

TIKI TWINKLES INTO LIFE

If you've ever sipped a Mai Tai or a Zombie, lounged under a palm-thatched roof or marveled at brightly colored fake Polynesian statues, then you've enjoyed the wonders of Tiki, a cocktail and nightlife genre that would never have been the same without Victor Bergeron. "Trader Vic" was born today in 1902, not on a South Pacific island as he occasionally claimed, but in downtown San Francisco. His business rival Donn Beach (Don the Beachcomber) may, in fact, have invented Tiki, inspired by his wanderings in the exotic South Seas—but it was Vic who took Donn Beach's concept to a new and global level, spawning a style of drink and decor that still catches eyes and palates today. Let's remember the man today with what is undisputedly one of his own creations, a Gun Club Punch No. 1.

Blue Mountain Cocktail

1½ shots aged rum • ½ shot vodka • ½ shot coffee liqueur • 1½ shots orange juice

Shake ingredients with ice and strain into chilled glass. Garnish with orange zest twist and coffee beans.

CELEBRATE THE MOUNTAINS

If you love mountains as much as we do, you'll be glad to know that today is International Mountain Day, a chance for us all to contemplate the role of mountains in our lives, from pristine climbing peaks and powder-rich ski resorts to rolling, forested hills. Mountains cover more than a quarter of the world's surface and are home to over 700 million people, while their forests capture fresh water for more than half the world's population. Today we are celebrating both their beauty and their utility with a Blue Mountain Cocktail, made with one of the finest coffees in the world, from Jamaica's Blue Mountains.

Jersey Sour

2 shots calvados • 1 shot lemon juice • ½ shot sugar syrup • ½ fresh egg white

Shake ingredients with ice and strain into chilled glass. Garnish with lemon zest twist.

OL' BLUE EYES BORN

Frank Sinatra, born today in 1915, sang, "I want to wake up, in a city that never sleeps/ And find I'm king of the hill/Top of the heap." He was from New Jersey but didn't let that hold him back. One of the most enduring musical icons of all time, and a successful actor, too, Sinatra married Ava Gardner and Mia Farrow and dated Marilyn Monroe, Lauren Bacall and Judy Garland. At the heart of the Rat Pack, a group of celebrities that made iconic their slouchy, suit-clad Vegas cool, Sinatra counted Humphrey Bogart and John F. Kennedy among his friends and partied as hard as he sang. The Jersey Sour, a timelessly classy blend of calvados and citrus, is enough to make anyone feel "top of the heap."

Creole Cosmo

1 shot rhum agricole • 1 shot Clément Creole Shrubb liqueur
1 shot cranberry juice • ½ shot lime juice

Shake ingredients with ice and strain into chilled glass. Garnish with lime zest twist.

NATIONAL DAY IN ST. LUCIA

Today in St. Lucia the sun, as always, shines and the good folks of this tiny country, a Caribbean island only 238 square miles in size and home to less than 200,000 people, are celebrating their independence with a nationwide party. Britain returned St. Lucia to the St. Lucians in 1979, having ruled it alternately with the French from the 17th century, and then controlling it from the early 19th century. Although the official language of St. Lucia is English, most locals still speak a form of French-based creole. So today why not celebrate the island and its people with an appropriately named drink, the Creole Cosmo?

Metropole

1½ shots Cognac V.S.O.P. • 1½ shots dry vermouth • 1 dash Peychaud's Bitters
1 dash orange bitters • ¼ shot maraschino cherry syrup (from cherry jar)

Stir ingredients with ice and strain into chilled glass. Garnish with maraschino cherry.

SOUTH POLE CONQUERED

The Norwegian explorer Roald Amundsen became the first human being to reach the South Pole on this day in 1911—an incredible feat that is sometimes overshadowed by the fate of his British competitor, Robert Falcon Scott, who arrived more than a month later and died in a blizzard only eleven miles from safety. Using Scandinavian efficiency—skis and well-organized supply depots—and survival skills he learned from Eskimos, including fur boots, reindeer-skin clothing, dogsleds, snowshoes, ice caves and igloos, Amundsen got himself and all his men safely through the most inhospitable environment on earth. We are toasting Amundsen's triumph with a Metropole, a vintage classic based on brandy, which he, like Scott, kept handy on his journey.

Brandy Blazer

2 shots Cognac V.S.O.P. • *2 shots boiling water* • *¼ shot sugar syrup (1 water : 2 sugar)*

Pour cognac into warmed glass and rest glass sideways on an old-fashioned glass. Flame the cognac and carefully move the glass upright onto your work surface. Pour in hot water (extinguish any remaining flame) and sugar. Stir and serve with a twist of lemon or orange. Garnish with lemon zest twist.

RIP, "PROFESSOR" JERRY THOMAS

Probably the first celebrity bartender and author of the first-known cocktail book, *Bartender's Guide*, "Professor" Jerry Thomas died in New York on this day in 1885. Since jumping ship in San Francisco to prospect for gold in the California hills, Thomas had been an art collector, a minstrel showman, an artist, a Freemason and more. He'd worked in New York, San Francisco, New Orleans, London and beyond, and had befriended gangsters, artists and boxers. A bartending impresario par excellence, complete with diamond tie pin, pet white rats and jeweled bar tools, he cultivated the image of a creative professional. His signature drink was the theatrical Blue Blazer, made with streams of blazing whiskey. We're suggesting you try a safer version: a Brandy Blazer.

Boston Deluxe

1½ shots bourbon whiskey • *¾ shot lemon juice* • *¾ shot orange juice*
½ shot saffron syrup • *2 dashes orange bitters* • *½ fresh egg white*

Dry shake ingredients. Shake again with ice and strain into chilled glass. Garnish with saffron fronds.

A TEA PARTY TO END AN EMPIRE

On this day in 1773, as the captains and crew of three British ships lay sleeping, more than a hundred men dressed as Native Americans, complete with tomahawks, crept into Boston harbor. Dividing into three groups, they stormed the ships, broke open the chests of tea the ships were carrying and scattered tea leaves, worth more than a million dollars in today's money, into the sea. The Boston Tea Party, one of many acts that would lead to American independence, had occurred. We are marking the anniversary not with tea but with a Boston Deluxe.

Biggles Aviation

2 shots London dry gin • ½ shot ginger liqueur • ½ shot lemon juice
¼ shot sugar syrup • ¼ shot cold water

Shake ingredients with ice and strain into chilled glass. Garnish with fresh ginger and lime slices.

WRIGHT TAKES TO THE SKIES

The world's first powered plane flight doesn't sound that impressive in raw numbers. When Orville Wright took to the skies on this day in 1903, he ascended to about first-story height above a South Carolina beach, and took a whole twelve seconds to fly less than 120 feet. Yet by the Wright brothers' fourth attempt on that selfsame gusty day, Orville's brother Wilbur had flown the plane for fifty-nine seconds over almost 984 feet. Powered flight, for centuries just a distant dream, was finally a reality. The Biggles Aviation, a take on the classic Aviation packed with seasonal ginger spice, makes the perfect drink to commemorate this anniversary. It's named for the fictional flying ace Biggles, who inspired a generation of British schoolboys.

Downhill Racer

1¾ shots light white rum • ¾ shot amaretto liqueur • 1¾ shots pineapple juice

Shake ingredients with ice and strain into chilled glass. Garnish with pineapple wedge.

FRANCE'S MOST FAMOUS WOMAN

Model, dancer and racing-car driver, Hellé Nice became France's most famous woman today in 1929, when she broke the world land-speed record for women by achieving 122.8 mph at Montlhéry in her lapis-blue Bugatti. A classic beauty who escaped from her small village to find fame, Hellé Nice not only was an outstanding athlete—she was also a trapeze artist and a skier—but raced F1 with the best, including the guys, and cut a swathe through some of her country's most eligible men. This bright and vibrant woman would die in poverty, forgotten, after a freak accident in 1936 ended her career. But we remember her today with an aptly named rum and amaretto confection, the Downhill Racer. Do join us.

Rose Memoire

2 teaspoons red currant jelly
1 shot clementine juice
3 shots rosé champagne

Shake first two ingredients with ice and strain into chilled glass. Top with champagne.

LITTLE SPARROW, BIG VOICE

A tiny, fragile-seeming chanteuse with the voice of a fallen angel, the woman who immortalized both "La Vie en Rose" and "Non, Je Ne Regrette Rien" was born on this day in 1915 into the sort of family of which depressing biographies are written. Abandoned by her junkie mother, Édith Piaf would grow up in her grandmother's brothel, learn stagecraft from her acrobat father, lose her only child when she was just nineteen, go through a bewildering cavalcade of lovers and, before her tragic and early death, become France's national diva and greatest international musical export. Even today the woman whose delicate frame gave her the nickname La Môme Piaf (the little sparrow) inspires movies, books and countless tribute recordings. We are celebrating her memory and her work with a Rose Memoire, a suitably classy cocktail based on elegant rosé champagne.

Vieux Carré

1 shot bourbon whiskey • 1 shot Cognac V.S.O.P. • ¼ shot Bénédictine D.O.M. liqueur • 1 shot sweet vermouth 1 dash bitters • 1 dash Peychaud's Bitters

Stir ingredients with ice and strain into ice-filled glass. Garnish with lemon zest twist.

BIGGEST PROPERTY DEAL EVER

Today in 1803 the French flag that had flown just briefly over La Nouvelle-Orléans was solemnly replaced with the Stars and Stripes, and the Louisiana territory belonged to the United States. For a mere $15 million, the U.S. acquired 828,000 square miles of land and doubled in size—not to mention taking official ownership of the spiritual home of the cocktail, New Orleans. In honor of the biggest property purchase ever, we are breaking out the crystal mixing glass and stirring up a 1930s New Orleans classic, the sweet yet splendidly complex Vieux Carré.

Doctor

1½ shots aged rum 1½ shots Swedish punch liqueur ¾ shot lime juice

Shake ingredients with ice and strain into chilled glass. Garnish with lime zest twist.

ENTER *THE DALEKS*

Exterminate!... Exterminate!... TV's most enduring bad guys, the Daleks, made their debut on this day in 1963. Those early Daleks, seen in this, their first series, doing battle with the Thals and the Ninth Doctor on their home planet, Skaro, would not unleash their famous cry until the fourth episode—although they did ultimately reveal their celebrated flaw, that vexatious inability to handle stairs. We are toasting *Doctor Who* in all its glorious incarnations with a suitably long-lived classic cocktail, the Doctor.

Cola de Mono

1 inch cinnamon stick 2 shots pisco 1 shot espresso coffee 1 shot coffee liqueur

Muddle cinnamon stick and pisco in base of shaker. Add other ingredients, shake with ice and strain into chilled glass. Garnish with cinnamon powder.

ANDES SURVIVORS FOUND

On October 13, 1972, a plane carrying rugby players to a match in Santiago, Chile, crashed high in the snowy Andes. More than two months later, long after everyone had given up hope, two men walked out of the mountains. They would lead rescuers to the remains of the plane and a further fourteen survivors, who had survived savage conditions in a triumph of the human spirit. In honor of the men who were rescued on this day we are drinking a Cola de Mono, an adaptation of a traditional Chilean drink, based on pisco, the spirit of the Andes.

Tom & Jerry

1 fresh egg (white and yolk) • *2 teaspoons superfine sugar* • *1 shot Cognac V.S.O.P.*
1 shot aged rum • *hot water*

Beat egg yolk and egg white separately in mixing bowls, then fold the yolk and white together with sugar. Stir in cognac and rum and pour into glass. Top with hot (not boiling) water, stir and serve. Garnish with freshly grated nutmeg.

A FESTIVUS FOR THE REST OF US

For *Seinfeld* obsessives, Festivus is Christmas. This fine celebration is based on the real-life family tradition of *Seinfeld* writer Dan O'Keefe and dates back to a 1997 episode of the show. For an authentic Festivus, replace the Christmas tree with an aluminum pole (no tinsel), formally air your grievances by telling all those around the table how much they have disappointed you, and then wrestle the head of the household to the ground. Festivus is a fabulous occasion to bring out one of the classic winter drinks, the Tom & Jerry, a meal in a glass that's perfect for sharing.

Chin Chin

½ teaspoon runny honey • *1 shot blended scotch whisky* • *½ shot apple juice* • *top with champagne brut*

Stir honey with scotch in base of shaker. Add apple juice, shake with ice and strain into chilled glass. Top with champagne.

THE NIGHT BEFORE CHRISTMAS

Today is, of course, Christmas Eve, and it's also, rather fabulously, the anniversary of the first time men orbited the moon. Yes, the three brave astronauts of the Apollo 8 mission spent Christmas Eve 1968 circling the moon no fewer than ten times, and capturing the iconic *Earthrise* photo to share with the rest of us. They were supplied with packaged turkey, gravy and cranberry sauce, but nothing by way of Christmas spirits, not even a bottle of champagne. Unlike the Apollo 8 astronauts, may we recommend you start Christmas off with a bang with a Chin Chin? Combining those two seasonal favorites, scotch whisky and champagne, with apple and a hint of honey, this very adult cocktail is Christmas in a glass.

Vavavoom

½ shot triple sec
½ shot lemon juice
½ shot sugar syrup
top with champagne brut

Pour ingredients into chilled glass.
Top with champagne.

A VERY MERRY CHRISTMAS TO YOU!

Merry Christmas and a Happy Birthday to the baby Jesus! Nobody really knows the exact date of Jesus's birthday, with some brave astronomers arguing that the Star of Wonder the Wise Men followed was actually a second-century conjunction of Jupiter and Venus sitting so close together that they looked like a single star. Whatever your religious affiliation, we hope you'll be enjoying the day with friends and family, and nothing says celebration quite like a round of champagne cocktails. Classics and fruit mixes have their time and place, but for Christmas entertaining we recommend the devilishly simple Vavavoom. When charged with a hint of orange liqueur, a little lemon and a soupçon of sugar, as it is in this recipe, even the humblest supermarket fizz will get your party going.

Wibble

1 shot London dry gin
1 shot sloe gin
1 shot pink grapefruit juice
¼ shot lemon juice
⅛ shot sugar syrup
⅛ shot crème de mûre

Shake ingredients with ice and strain into chilled glass.
Garnish with lemon zest twist.

BOXING DAY

Depending on where you're from, today is St. Stephen's Day, Boxing Day, Wren Day or just the day after Christmas. St. Stephen himself was an early martyr, stoned to death in Jerusalem for praising Jesus in front of a skeptical audience; St. Stephen's Day is, of course, the day on which Good King Wenceslas went to help a poor peasant with his firewood; and it's quite likely that a tradition of giving alms to the poor, Wenceslas-style, gave Boxing Day its name. Wren Day, meanwhile, is a long-standing tradition in some Celtic parts of Europe, where people hunt real or fake wrens. Whether you're hunting wrens or simply peace and quiet, take a tip from rural Britons, who traditionally drink sloe gin today, and discover the Wibble, a genuinely world-class cocktail based on that classic winter warmer.

Peter Pan Martini

1 shot London dry gin • 1 shot dry vermouth • 1 shot orange juice • 3 dashes peach bitters

Shake ingredients with ice and strain into chilled glass. Garnish with orange zest twist.

PETER PAN COMES TO LONDON

The personification of eternal youth, the ultimate boy who wouldn't grow up, Peter Pan made his stage debut in London's Duke of York theater today back in 1904, the brainchild of Scottish journalist-turned-playwright J. M. Barrie. With Captain Hook and Tinkerbell, he's proved enduringly popular ever since, showing that *Peter Pan* was a much better title than one of Barrie's earlier attempts, *The Boy Who Hated Mothers*. Whatever you make of Barrie himself—among other misdemeanors he forged a female friend's will to enable him to adopt her five young orphaned boys—his creation has endured. We are celebrating Peter Pan, and the inner child in all of us, with a Peter Pan Martini.

Merry-Go-Round Martini

2 shots London dry gin • ½ shot dry vermouth • ½ shot sweet vermouth

Stir ingredients with ice and strain into chilled glass. Garnish with olive or lemon zest twist.

DÍA DE LOS SANTOS INOCENTES

Herod the Great doesn't have the best press in Christian literature, what with allegedly massacring every young male child in Bethlehem. Today Spaniards and many Latin Americans remember his activities with Day of the Holy Innocents, the Spanish-speaking world's answer to April Fool's Day. The media run spoof stories, kids play pranks, bonfires are lit and in some villages children get to play mayor for the day. Across Spain, Alicante sees flour battles in the streets, Fraga folks throw eggs at one another, Tremp people burn a giant paper doll, and Valencia kids dress up for the Dance of the Fools. A Merry-Go-Round Martini, a martini blended with two different vermouths, sums it all up.

Gin Atomic

*3 fresh basil leaves • 2 shots London dry gin • 1 shot elderflower liqueur • ½ shot lemon juice
2 dashes lemon bitters • top with tonic water*

Lightly muddle (just to bruise) basil in base of shaker. Add other ingredients except for tonic, shake with ice and strain into ice-filled glass. Top with tonic water. Garnish with lemon zest twist.

GENIUS DREAMS UP NANOTECH

Nanotechnology, the science of manipulating incredibly tiny things—like atoms and molecules—truly awe-inspiring. Scientists have made films by positioning individual atoms and two physicis won a Nobel Prize for their work on sheets of carbon so thin they're basically two-dimensional. Th amazing concept was first outlined today in 1959, when physics genius Richard Feynman explained to a rap audience how the Encyclopedia Britannica really could be written on the head of a pin. If you like the ide of a future where molecule-size robots race through our bloodstreams curing everything from hangovers t cancer, this is one idea worth celebrating, and the Gin Atomic strikes a suitably atom-scaled note.

José Collins

2 shots tequila • 1 shot lemon juice • ½ shot sugar syrup • top with soda

Shake first three ingredients with ice and strain into ice-filled glasses. Top with soda and stir.
Garnish with orange slice and maraschino cherry.

RIZAL DAY

Every December 30, men and women across the Philippines celebrate Rizal Day in honor of their national hero, José Rizal. Executed by Spanish troops on the penultimate day of 1896 at the age of only thirty-five, Rizal was a polymath: an artist, poet, writer, fencer and more. He studied medicine, specializing in ophthalmology so that he could cure his mother's incipient blindness; started a school; invented brick-making machines; and campaigned for Filipino nationhood, freedom and education. The last poem he wrote before his death, "My Last Farewell," was read by Indonesian soldiers going into battle for their freedom five decades later. Filipinos may fly their flags at half-mast today, but we are toasting José's legacy with an aptly named José Collins.

Grape Escape

8 white grapes
5 fresh mint leaves
2 shots Cognac V.S.O.P.
½ shot sugar syrup
top with champagne brut

Muddle grapes and mint in base of shaker. Add cognac and sugar, shake with ice and strain into glass filled with crushed ice. Top with champagne and stir. Garnish with mint.

NEW YEAR'S EVE

Tonight the world will be celebrating the New Year. In New York, it's all about the ball drop; in Sydney and Hong Kong, fireworks rule; in London, jumping into a fountain remains mystifyingly popular; the civilized Spanish eat twelve grapes, to bring good luck for each month of the new year. The choice of an appropriate drink for New Year's Eve is every bit as important as those resolutions you'll be making on New Year's Day—and let's face it, a lot more pleasurable, too. You may consider Champagne Cocktails, meddle with Mimosas, or flirt with Fizzes, but the Grape Escape, a blend of champagne, cognac, fresh mint and fresh grapes, is the sort of subtly gorgeous fizzy thing that should start any New Year off on the very best possible terms. Happy New Year!

ABOUT THE AUTHOR

Simon Difford is a man who lives and breathes the modern drinks industry. His own bar, at his South London home, is one of the best stocked in the world, containing practically every example of category spirits and liqueurs on the market today. He has become a world authority and expert on distillation, and is respected for his encyclopedic knowledge on numerous spirit categories.

Simon established Difford's Guide in 2001. Since then, the brand has become a global authority on cocktail culture. The Difford's Guide website, diffordsguide.com, is one of the world's largest and most visited drinks-related websites. In addition to the website, Difford's Guide also publishes a series of drinks-related guide books, with *Difford's Guide to Cocktails* now in its eleventh edition, which is perhaps the most well known. Both this book and diffordsguide.com carry recipes for more than 3,000 cocktails, and Simon has personally made every drink to test it, and in many cases improved the recipe.

Difford's Guide has been recognized and awarded many times for its work on everything from bar reviews to product tastings and lifestyle content. In 2013, Difford's Guide won Best Cocktail Writing (publication) at Tales of Cocktail in New Orleans.